Count Your Blessings

Other Hay House Titles by Dr. John F. Demartini

The Breakthrough Experience: A Revolutionary New Approach to Personal Transformation

How to Make One Hell of a Profit and Still Get to Heaven

You Can Have an Amazing Life . . . in Just 60 Days!

All of the above are available at your local bookstore,
or may be ordered by visiting:

Hay House USA: **www.hayhouse.com**®
Hay House Australia: **www.hayhouse.com.au**
Hay House UK: **www.hayhouse.co.uk**
Hay House South Africa: **orders@psdprom.co.za**
Hay House India: **www.hayhouseindia.co.in**

Count Your Blessings

The Healing Power of Gratitude and Love

Dr. John F. Demartini

HAY HOUSE, INC.
Carlsbad, California
London • Sydney • Johannesburg
Vancouver • Hong Kong • Mumbai

Published and distributed in the United States by: Hay House, Inc.: www.hayhouse.
com • **Published and distributed in Australia by:** Hay House Australia Pty. Ltd.: www.
hayhouse.com.au • **Published and distributed in the United Kingdom by:** Hay House
UK, Ltd.: www.hayhouse.co.uk • **Published and distributed in the Republic of South
Africa by:** Hay House SA (Pty), Ltd.: orders@psdprom.co.za • **Distributed in Canada
by:** Raincoast: www.raincoast.com • **Published in India by:** Hay House Publications
(India) Pvt. Ltd.: www.hayhouseindia.co.in • **Distributed in India by:** Media Star:
booksdivision@mediastar.co.in

Design: Bryn Starr Best

Originally published by Element Books in 1997: ISBN: 0 00 715813 0

Library of Congress Cataloging-in-Publication Data

Demartini, John F.
  Count your blessings : the healing power of gratitude and love / John F. Demartini.
    p. cm.
  Originally published: Rockport, Mass. : Element, 1997.
  Includes bibliographical references (p.254).
  ISBN-13: 978-1-4019-1074-7 (tradepaper)
  ISBN-10: 1-4019-1074-2 (tradepaper)
  1. Gratitude. 2. Love. 3. Mind and body. 4. Spiritual life. I. Title.
  BF575.G68D46 2006
  158.1--dc22

                                    2005029085

                        ISBN 13: 978-1-4019-1074-7
                        ISBN 10: 1-4019-1074-2

                        09 08 07 06   4 3 2 1
                        1st Hay House printing, June 2006

                    Printed in the United States of America

*This book is dedicated to all individuals
who would love to heal their minds,
bodies, and lives through the power
of gratitude and unconditional love.*

Contents

Preface

I do not know what I may appear to the world,
but to myself I seem to have been only like a boy
playing on the seashore and diverting myself
in now and then finding a smoother pebble
or a prettier shell than ordinary whilst the great
ocean of truth lay all undiscovered before me.
— Isaac Newton

When I was a young boy, my parents encouraged me to be grateful for my health, my life, and all the world's wonders. They would often remind me to count my blessings, and over time it became a part of my everyday life. When I began studying and then practicing as a professional the principles of healing, I observed a strong link between gratitude, love, and healing. I began focusing my research in this area more than 15 years ago and continue to be inspired by each healing principle I discover.

Each connection I find between gratitude, love, and healing is like a sparkling star of light, a perfect pebble in the stream of consciousness. And each day I awake with a sense of anticipation that I may discover another principle of health—another inspirational story of healing—to share with others. That's why I founded the Concourse of Wisdom School of Philosophy and Healing. It's also why I created "The Demartini Method," and why I've written this book.

The many principles and stories I'm able to share with you create a foundation for living a healthy and fulfilling life just by tapping in to the power of gratitude and love. When you apply these principles, you reap the benefits of healing your mind and body, following the wisdom of your heart and soul, and experiencing the most powerful force in existence—the power of gratitude and love.

Each principle and story will help you take another step toward healing those conditions in your life that you'd love to heal, and make quantum leaps in your personal and spiritual development, as you walk along your unique and special journey.

Chapter 1

Gratitude and Love Are the Heart of Healing

Miracles do not happen in contradiction with nature,
but in contradiction with what we know about nature.
— Saint Augustine

Do You Have the Heart to Heal Yourself?

We all have the healing power of unconditional love within us. But we sometimes unwisely believe that we can't be healed. When we're sick, it's easy to listen to our fears, and tempting to put all our efforts into tangible, physical remedies that we can see and touch. But if we want a more complete and lasting healing, we must take a step beyond what we can merely see or touch, and listen to the inner wisdom of our hearts and souls as well.

This inner wisdom, expressing itself through gratitude and unconditional love, is the most powerful healing force there is. No condition, illness, or disease exists that can't be helped by its pure energy. We can interpret *incurable* to mean, simply, curable from within! And when we're

1

grateful for what is, as it is, our hearts open and speak to us with healing messages. These are the moments when we inwardly hear the guidance of our hearts and souls. Being grateful and opening our hearts to unconditional love is the essence of healing.

This same essence creates spontaneous healing—what some call miracles—when we intensify its power by being completely present and having total certainty that healing can and will occur. The most inspired healers know that the power that made the body can heal the body, and they share this certainty with their patients. They also know that in numerous instances, internal forces have healed conditions and diseases that had been diagnosed as irreparable or terminal simply because there were no known externally administered, traditional remedies or cures. But when we limit ourselves to physical treatments and remedies, we don't reap the benefits of the unlimited source of healing that's within us.

I'm grateful for the opportunity to share other people's personal stories of healing because they serve as reminders of what truly is possible. Believing that we can make ourselves well is a vital part of the healing process. Sometimes people block the healing power of unconditional love when they feel they don't deserve to heal, or when they hold on to anger or other unbalanced emotions. For example, Angie, a former chiropractic patient of mine, came to me after her neck and back were injured in a car accident. She was a gymnast and was on her way to a performance when a van hit the passenger side of her car. Angie spent several days in the hospital and several weeks resting at home, but she wasn't seeing any improvement in her condition. "I haven't gotten any of my flexibility back. I still can't turn my head, and my back feels as stiff as a board," she explained.

I asked Angie to tell me about the collision, and she began to describe the events as she recalled them. As she spoke, her voice became louder and faster, her face flushed with emotion. She said she was very angry, and she was afraid she was going to miss months of competition and performance. "Why did this happen to me?" she asked. As she spoke, I could see Angie's body tensing and becoming even more rigid. I realized that she might be blocking her own healing with her anger and ingratitude. I explained that if she balanced her emotions concerning the accident, she could open her heart and begin to benefit from the healing essence of unconditional love. "What do you mean, 'when I balance my emotions'?" she asked. "I can't help how I feel!"

I explained that our emotions are based on our perceptions. The fact that we can, and do, change our minds and our opinions indicates that we can also change our perceptions and the way we feel about things. "Okay," she said, "but what does that have to do with healing my neck so I can perform again?" I suggested to Angie that the anger she felt surrounding her injury might be creating a block in her healing and explained that by balancing her perceptions she could exchange anger for gratefulness and the healing power of unconditional love. She agreed that it was worth trying and said she would return the following day.

When Angie arrived, I explained the method I call "The Demartini Method," which I developed to help balance perception and tap in to unconditional love. For the next few hours, Angie worked on balancing her perceptions of the collision, the driver of the van, and her injury. She eventually discovered that an equal number of negatives and positives were associated with the car wreck, the other driver, and even her own injury. She could see how she had done to other people the same types of things that she now accused the driver of doing to her. And she realized that she wanted to stop blaming and start healing.

When Angie completed the final step in The Demartini Method, she looked up at me with tears in her eyes and said, "Wow! I *can* help how I feel. I really get it. Blaming doesn't help anything. Right now, I feel really grateful just to be alive." I asked Angie to step into the adjusting room and focus on her gratefulness and on her vision of the flexibility she was certain to regain. I then adjusted her and asked her to remain in a relaxed state for a moment or two after the adjustment to feel the unconditional love healing her neck and her back. As she sat up gradually and then stood, I could see that she already had regained some of her flexibility. She confirmed what I saw. "I can actually turn my head a little," she said with a big smile. I supported Angie's internal healing process with several more adjustments and exactly one month after her completion of The Demartini Method, she won a gymnastic competition for a routine she performed on the balance beam.

All Complete Healing Is Activated
Through Love and Gratitude

> *Love cures people, the ones who receive love*
> *and the ones who give it, too.*
> — Karl A. Menninger

- Unconditional love heals.

- True, heartfelt gratitude releases unconditional love.

- The power that made the body can heal the body.

- No matter what healers or therapists do, they can only support your own natural or inherent healing processes.

Sickness and suffering actually function as hidden blessings, because they smash our complacency concerning the fictions we've developed about our lives and force us to be present in our lives. Sometimes an injury or disease awakens our love for life. Few situations urge us to examine our life more than the possibility of our impending death. For many people, including our loved ones, the day they're diagnosed with a life-threatening illness is the day they truly begin to live and appreciate life.

This was the case for a lovely woman named Josephine who shared her inspirational story with me a few years ago. She was 77 when I met her and is still one of the most vital people I know. She exudes energy and has such love and spark that her eyes twinkle, and she almost seems to glow. Her story began when she was in her late 50s. Doctors determined that she had a malignant brain tumor and scheduled surgery for a few days later. She was instructed to go home and rest in the meantime. "Those three days were the worst, and the best, days of my life," Josephine said.

I sat out on the back-porch swing and listened to the birds sing and reviewed my life. I knew that somehow my frequent anger and frustration, and all the times I behaved in an unloving manner, had added up to that moment. I laughed and I cried, and I realized that the events in my life that seemed so awful when they were happening often led to something beneficial down the road. And it occurred to me that perhaps—somehow—that was true for my tumor as well.

Josephine contacted her family members and asked them to please come see her. While she waited for their arrival, she wrote each of them a letter thanking them for all the love they had shown her, for all the thoughtful favors they had done, and for the many gifts they had given her throughout the years. They all arrived the day before her scheduled operation, accompanied her to the hospital the following day, and shared stories and laughed until visiting hours were over.

When everyone had gone, as Josephine looked out her window at the stars, she began to be thankful for all her blessings. She was so filled with love that tears of gratitude streamed down her face. She recalls:

> I felt completely immersed in love, and I felt a complete sense of inner peace. Then I thought I saw a light go on behind me, and I turned around to see what looked like a beautiful young woman with long, flowing hair smiling at me and radiating with light. She said she was an angel who felt my love, and she had come to reassure me that everything would be okay; that I would have plenty of time to fulfill my life's purpose. And then she said, "Always remember that it was your love and your appreciation that brought healing to you, Josephine. You are blessed." I closed my eyes when she hugged me, and when I opened them, she was gone.

Josephine spent the rest of the night wide awake, thinking about what had happened, and wondering what her life's purpose was. As she thought about what she'd really love to do, she realized that she wanted to be a counselor or therapist, and she decided that she'd begin applying to colleges in order to fulfill this dream.

When morning came and Josephine's children arrived, she told them that she no longer needed to have the operation and asked them to take her home. Her doctor strongly advised her against leaving, but she insisted. She promised that she'd return in a few months for a checkup and would call him if she had any problems. By the time Josephine returned for her exam, her energy and vitality had returned, and her doctor and her family celebrated when they learned that the tumor, which had been slightly smaller than a golf ball, had miraculously disappeared.

Certainty and Presence Intensify Healing

*The person who says it cannot be done
should not interrupt the person doing it.*
— Chinese proverb

- Be certain that you will heal.

- Visualize yourself doing what you love to do, and believe you will do these things again when you are well.

- Fill your heart with so many grateful thoughts that no room remains for worry and fear.

- Be present to the healing energy of unconditional love.

Being certain that you'll heal, and being present to the guidance of your heart and soul, can enhance your healing process. Doubts and fears cause you to tune out your own inner wisdom and block the flow of healing energy, but having gratitude for what is—as it is—accelerates and intensifies your healing.

A few years ago I was gifted with the opportunity to help a man named Michael, a dancer who'd been paralyzed from his neck down as the result of an injury. Before he suffered the injury, I'd treated him a few times for minor sprains and strains. His dream was to dance in Broadway productions, and he was devastated by his paralysis. Michael could still move his head and arms, but he believed it when he was told that he'd never walk again. He lost interest in trying to improve and was beginning to lose his ability to speak clearly. He truly had a broken body and a broken heart.

When he arrived at my office in his wheelchair, his head hung down so far that we couldn't make eye contact. I could see that he'd nearly given up, so I got down in front of him, took his hands in mine, looked into his eyes, and said, "Michael, if you lose your vision and your dream, you'll lose your will to live, and you may never get out of this wheelchair.

"You have to see light at the end of the tunnel. You must be able to comprehend that you'll walk again. You have to see yourself dancing. You have to see yourself on stage, Michael. You must see yourself healed. You have to picture it . . . if you can't picture it, your physiology can't create it. Even if it seems impossible right now, you have to see the impossible becoming possible."

He started to cry. "I just want to walk," he said. "I just want to be able to walk. Why do I have to go through this?"

"This is a gift," I told him, "and until you can see it as a gift, it will hold you back. There is no crisis without a blessing; there is no turmoil without a gift."

I gave Michael a special videotape and told him to watch it as many times as it took for him to see light at the end of the tunnel; to see himself walking and dancing. I said, "You have to hold in your mind's eye a virtual reality that's greater than your physical reality." And he cried and put his arm on my shoulder; he pulled me toward him and we held each other. At that moment, he saw light at the end of the tunnel. With tears in his eyes, he said, "I'm gonna walk again."

The videotape I gave Michael was about Morris Goodman, who is called the "Miracle Man." After surviving a plane crash that broke almost every bone in his body—including his skull—and resulted in his becoming paralyzed, he eventually learned to walk again. His story is one of the most inspirational stories of healing I know.

When Morris was first taken to the hospital, no one believed he'd live. But he did. Although in a coma, he kept hanging on. His family knew that he enjoyed Zig Ziglar and his philosophy of life, so they brought in a tape recorder and played Ziglar's tapes and inspirational messages over and over again for Morris. When I met him, Morris told me that while he was in the coma, he was aware and could hear the tapes. He decided to focus on willing himself to move his eye and one of his fingers. He said he spent three weeks visualizing himself moving his finger and winking his eye. Then, one day, when the nurse was in the room, he was able to wink his eye, and she saw it. The following day he moved his finger, which the nurse also saw. He told me that he was trying to communicate so the doctors and his family wouldn't give up on him. Over the next few months, his body started to function again, and eventually he walked out of the hospital.

I told Michael to watch this documentary about the Miracle Man over and over between adjustments. He did this for about three months, but still no significant changes were occurring. It was becoming difficult, even for me, to maintain my vision of hope and my certainty that he would heal because I wasn't seeing any progress. Then one day, when I walked in to adjust Michael, I had a yearning to adjust his neck. He had wires and bolts in his neck, but my voice of intuition and inspiration said that adjusting his neck would help. I realized that I had been letting my own fear hold me back. So I listened to my inner voice of inspiration and adjusted his neck. That night he moved his toes.

I made a commitment to myself that from then on, when the inner voice of my heart and soul inspired and guided me, I'd listen and obey.

I continued to adjust Michael, and day by day, little by little, he improved. In less than a year, he was able to stand up and balance himself. He held on to his dream and kept his focus on the light at the end of the tunnel until one Monday when I saw Michael in the reception room, he stood up, took two steps toward me, and fell into my arms. Over the next few years, Michael became able to retire his wheelchair and dance at his own party.

The Truth Is . . .

Every truth passes through three stages before it is recognized.
In the first it is ridiculed; in the second it is opposed;
in the third it is regarded as self-evident.
— Arthur Schopenhauer

- The power that made the body can heal the body.

- Incurable means curable from within.

- Gratitude and unconditional love activate a more profound and complete healing.

- Certainty and presence intensify unconditional love's healing energy.

- There is no healing force greater than unconditional love.

Reflections

Natural forces within us are the true healers of disease.
— Hippocrates

1. Close your eyes and visualize the condition or illness you'd love to heal.

2. Think of all the ways that condition or illness has—and is—benefiting you.

3. Visualize the energy of unconditional love filling every cell of your body and healing you completely.

4. Be certain that you will be healed.

Realizations

1. Write down the condition or illness that you'd love to heal.

2. Next, in a column, write down all the drawbacks of the condition. Then, in another column, write an equal number of ways that the condition or illness is serving, or is of benefit to, you.

3. Make a list of the things you plan to do when you're well.

4. Write a thank-you letter to yourself for seeing the balance in your situation or illness. Humble yourself and open your heart to the healing essence of gratitude and unconditional love.

Affirmations

*   *I am grateful for my condition as it is.*

*   *I am opening my heart to the healing essence of unconditional love.*

*   *I am grateful, and certain, that I am healing.*

*   *I am healing my body and my mind.*

Chapter 2

Be Grateful for Your Broken Heart

*All I have seen teaches me to trust the
creator for all I have not seen.*
— Ralph Waldo Emerson

Have You Counted the Blessings of Your Broken Heart?

Have you counted the blessings of your broken heart? Just because you can't see the blessings of your heartache doesn't mean they're not there. The events and circumstances in our lives that offer the most heartache also offer the greatest opportunities to experience the magnificence of unconditional love and the perfection of the universe. And the truth is, there's no such thing as a "broken heart." The emotion we refer to as a broken heart is just a result of the imaginary void and resentment we feel when an illusion of infatuation is shattered, or when we think we've lost something or someone. These unbalanced illusions can make us sick if we don't balance them with gratitude and unconditional love.

If you're attached to the illusion that someone you love will always be physically present in your life, you may have a very difficult time when this person departs physically— either at the end of a relationship, or by stepping through the doorway some call death. But when you open your heart to the blessings of your experience, you can benefit from every transition and transformation that occurs in your life. Remember, you are the master of your fate and the captain of your soul.

As we travel through life and take on the challenges of difficult experiences, love dissolves our illusions and gives us greater strength. I'll always remember consulting with a man who was in the process of separating from his wife, to whom he'd been married 23 years. He was experiencing so much sorrow that he was having a hard time functioning in his daily life. He said, "I can't believe she's leaving me after all these years. I thought we'd always be together. What am I going to do all alone for the rest of my life?"

William was experiencing the shattering of his illusion that Marge would always be a physical presence in his life. He felt let down and despondent, and his energy level was very low. For the next hour or so, I helped William see that his divorce was not "all bad," and he began to acknowledge that he'd been overlooking a few benefits— such as golfing as much as he wanted and staying out as late as he felt like, without calling Marge for her approval. Once he acknowledged these two benefits, he began to see a host of others, and before long he found 53 blessings in what he had originally seen only as heartbreak.

Broken Illusions Are Blessings

To see your drama clearly is to be liberated from it.
— Ken Keyes, Jr.

- Illusions block the path to truth.

- Unconditional love is the core of all truth.

- When your heart is open, no one is "missing."

- Every shattered illusion reveals a benefit.

Every time we experience a broken illusion, we have the opportunity to experience a truth. When we reserve judgment about a person or situation, we express our certainty that the benefits equal the drawbacks, even if we have yet to see the perfect balance. When we think a person or a situation is more "bad" than "good," or more "good" than "bad," we block the truth with our lopsided view.

The emotional pain and physical illness you may experience when someone physically exits your life is often intensified by your misconception that the person who left has something you imagine you lack. But the truth is, you have that "special something" within yourself! The key is to discover it.

Sheila is a person who was very upset when her father died. They had a very close relationship, and she felt that a part of her died with her father. I explained to her that her father's true essence is just as present now as it was when it was in his physical body. I said, "Just because you can't see and touch your father doesn't mean that he no longer exists." Her look of confusion brought me to explain, "Sheila, nothing and no one can truly be destroyed. When you heat an ice cube, it turns to water. If you continue heating that water, it turns to steam. The essence of the ice cube remains; just the form is different."

"But that doesn't do me any good when I want to talk to him! I miss him, Dr. Demartini. I can't handle the idea that I can never talk to him again," she said as she began to cry.

"Sheila," I asked, "what did your father say to you when you were grieving the death of one of your friends?"

She smiled and said, "When my best friend Ellen died of cancer a few years ago, he put his hands on my shoulders, looked me straight in the eyes, and said, 'Sheila, I believe I taught you that when God welcomes a new angel, everyone is blessed. '"

I explained to Sheila that nothing was preventing her from continuing to talk to her father, and even to hear his answers in her mind. "I think I can see that now," she said, "but what can I do to stop feeling so much like I miss him?" I knew that when Sheila really felt grateful for the lessons and blessings of her father's passing, her heart would open to unconditional love and she'd immediately feel her father's love as well. Step by step, I took Sheila through The Demartini Method, and step by step, she began to appreciate the blessings of her sorrow. When she finally completed the Method, she felt her father's presence and thanked him for being such an important part of her life, saying that she felt his eternal love for her in her heart. Then she thanked me for the opportunity to experience love on such a profound level, and said she felt comforted to know that death was just a transformation and her father was still with her.

Every Joy Has Its Sorrow; Every Sorrow Has Its Joy

Your joy is your sorrow unmasked.
And the selfsame well from which your laughter rises
was oftentimes filled with your tears.
— Kahlil Gibran

- Circumstances may be likened to stones—you can use them to build on, or you can let them weigh you down.

- Each trial is a potential doorway to unconditional love.

- Joy and sorrow push you to grow and expand to a greater concentric sphere of influence, responsibility, and reward. Experiences of emotional pain are opportunities to learn love.

Even the deepest, darkest sorrows have an equal amount of joy—the sooner we find it, the sooner we experience the blessings. Every lesson we're given is an opportunity to experience a new level of unconditional love. When we embrace the lesson, we allow the blessings to unfold gracefully. Often when we reject the lesson, we get stuck in the cycle of ingratitude, and block the love and truth trying to flow through our lives.

I remember the way a woman named Monica glowed with love's light when she was able to release her anger and her sorrow over her son's death and embrace him through unconditional love. Monica's ten-year-old son, Lenny, had been killed in a drive-by shooting just a few months before she attended my personal growth and success program called The Breakthrough Experience. She introduced herself at the beginning of the program by saying, "My name is Monica, and I'm here because I want to heal my broken heart."

She said that she was struggling with every aspect of Lenny's death, but what bothered her most was how meaningless and senseless it all seemed to be. "Why did my son have to die for nothing?" she asked. I told Monica that, while we may not always be able to see the perfection and balance of a situation, it's always there waiting to be discovered and loved.

Later that afternoon when we began The Demartini Method, Monica was surprised to see how many blessings had already arisen from Lenny's death. A volunteer neighborhood crime-watch program had been organized, and the visibility of law enforcement had increased in her area. In addition, donations were being collected to build a basketball court in Lenny's memory at the neighborhood park. She had received prayers, cards, food, and support from people she didn't even know. One card in particular touched her heart. She pulled this card out of her purse, from a woman with five children of her own, and read it aloud:

Dear Monica,

I saw the story of your son's death on the evening news, and as I sat with tears in my eyes thinking of the sorrow you must feel, I realized it had been a while since I hugged each one of my kids and told them that I loved them. I appreciate the message of love that your son's death sent to me and to hundreds of other parents just like me. Thank you.

By the end of The Demartini Method, Monica could clearly appreciate the blessings of her son's life, and of his death. She said, "As much as it has hurt to finally reach this point of understanding, the pain I've suffered is worth the ten years of love I was able to share with Lenny. He's my angel son now, and I feel his love with every beat of my heart."

The Truth Is . . .

There cannot be day without night,
joy without sorrow,
nor spring without winter.
— Zula Bennington Greene

- Your one true being or soul loves, and is grateful for, what is—as it is.

- One of your greatest gifts is your desire to love and be loved.

- You are here to love and be loved, not to be "right."

- Your sorrow shows you what you haven't yet learned to love.

Reflections

What was hard to endure can be sweet to recall.
— Occidental proverb

1. Recall a shattered illusion you've experienced.

2. Take a few moments to review the benefits that resulted from that shattered illusion.

3. Think of a situation about which you feel sorrowful.

4. Think of at least three joys that arose out of your sorrow.

Realizations

The mind is its own place, and in it self,
Can make a Heav'n of Hell, a Hell of Heav'n.
— John Milton

1. On a sheet of paper, write the name or initials of the person about whom you are "heartbroken."

2. Now, list 20 blessings and 20 drawbacks associated with the person and with your perception of "losing" them.

3. Write a letter to the person thanking them for the benefits of your experience.

4. Write an entry in your journal, or a thank-you letter to someone you love, expressing your love and gratitude for the perfection and magnificence of your life and the universe.

Affirmations

- *My inner voice brings balance to my perceptions of heartbreak and brightens my heart with love, wisdom, and power.*

- *I am shattering my illusions and experiencing the blessings of the healing truth.*

- *I am grateful for the lessons and blessings of my heartaches.*

- *I am healing my broken illusions with gratitude and love.*

Chapter 3

Do What You Love, and Love What You Do

You are never given a wish without also
being given the power to make it come true.
You may have to work for it, however.
— Richard Bach

Do You Suffer from the Monday-Morning Blues?

It's amazing how many people begin their day—not with a sense of inspiration, but with resignation, depression, and even desperation. Their alarm clock rings, and instead of leaping out of bed filled with thankfulness for another day of life, their thoughts plummet into despair as they realize that their day is filled with tasks labeled *Must Do*— none of which are things that they love to do!

Statistics reveal that many people feel so despondent about getting up and facing their daily toils and responsibilities that more people suffer from heart attacks at seven o'clock on Monday morning than at any other time of the week. This could be termed the "Monday-morning heart-attack blues." And if that many people are having heart attacks from the thought of work, imagine how many people are making themselves sick in other ways.

The irony is that it's just as simple to fill your day with things you love to do as it is to fill your day with things you must do, need to do, or dread doing! We sometimes forget that we have the power to create the life we love. In fact, when we listen to the wisdom of our intuition, or inner voice, we discover that we're most fulfilled when we're doing what we love, and loving what we do.

That's what we're designed to do! When we trust and follow our inner voice, we remember that each day is a gift, and we make a commitment to appreciate that gift by working toward what we love.

Several years ago at a networking conference, a young man shared one of his dreams: to make a video that would teach women makeup techniques that could help them look and feel their best. Michael was a talented cosmetic stylist, and his voice conveyed such inspiration that I told him I was certain he could achieve his dream.

He was curious why I was so sure, so he invited me to lunch to find out. During our lunch meeting, I explained to him that when people do what they love to do, their inspiration creates an internal drive toward success. "Most people are caught in the illusion that they have to complete certain things, or reach a particular age or income level before they can start doing what they love to do." Michael agreed that he saw that cycle in his own life and in his friends' lives.

People say things such as, "After I make more contacts, then I can start my own business," or "Once my kids go to college, then I can do some of the things I've dreamed about," or "When I retire, then I'll have time to do what I'd really love to do." I told Michael that we can either make excuses or we can make our dreams come true. The choice is ours, and the secret is to determine what we love to do and begin doing it!

"I'm definitely going to pursue this video," he said, "but I have to make a living, too. I can't quit my job to do what I love to do, can I?" I told Michael that learning to love what he's doing now would help him to do more of what he loves. "It's not just a matter of doing what you love, it's also loving what you do," I explained.

"But I'm totally bored with the daily grind," he said. "How can I learn to love my job?" I suggested to Michael that he list 30 things about his job that he liked and 30 things he didn't like. Then I said he should look at how doing each item on his list helps prepare him to do more of what he is inspired about doing.

About a month later, Michael attended The Break-through Experience. Here he clearly defined a vision, inspiration, and purpose for his life. His dreams were to own and operate a cosmetics company, produce the cosmetics instructional video, write ten books in ten years, be instrumental in healing, and write and produce music. Today Michael has a video and an infomercial to his credit, he has written six of his ten books, his music is in the hands of a promising agent in Nashville, and he's helping others open their hearts to healing their lives.

Doing What You Love Is the Key to Fulfillment

If one advances confidently in the direction of his dreams,
and endeavors to live the life which he has imagined,
he will meet with a success unexpected in common hours.
— Henry David Thoreau

- You are designed to do what you love.

- Your primary purpose is to follow your inspirations and fulfill what you love.

- When you link your daily actions to your purpose, you live the life you love.

- When you do what you love, and love what you do, you find yourself openhearted and thankful, and your inner voice speaks to you and guides you.

The more you do what you love and love what you do, the more fulfilling your entire life becomes. For example, about five years ago an Australian woman named Barbara was vacationing in Quebec when she heard two men in a coffee shop talking about The Breakthrough Experience. A few days later, Barbara called me to inquire about the program. She explained that although she was shy and it was unlike her to approach people she didn't know, something compelled her to find out more about the program. She was so intrigued by the idea of learning how she could do what she loved that she extended her vacation an extra week and came to the next Breakthrough program.

Barbara was a prominent attorney who had just been offered a partnership in her firm. She said that it was exactly what she'd been working toward for years, but now that the opportunity was knocking, she wasn't sure if she wanted to open the door and let it in. She said that she'd been thinking a lot about her old dreams—the ones she'd dismissed as unrealistic when she decided to follow in her father's footsteps and go to law school.

"I put so much time and energy into all of this. How come I'm not fulfilled? How can I even think about wasting all the work I've already accomplished to try something I don't even know if I can do?" she asked.

With a little encouragement, Barbara revealed that the dream she had dismissed was to be an artist. She said that she loved to paint portraits and had been painting since she was a child, although she hadn't done much of it during the past ten years. "When I get out my paints, I feel exhilarated at first, but then I get really depressed because I know it'll never be more than a hobby," she explained.

I asked Barbara a few questions to help her focus on her inspirations and her vision of the life she'd love to be living. As she looked deeper into her thoughts and beliefs, she realized that she could begin pursuing her dream without giving up the security of her current position . . . until she was ready to take that step.

She stayed with the law firm but turned down the partnership. Within two years, she was earning so much money from her work painting portraits that she was able to leave her full-time position and work as a legal consultant. Today her paintings sell in some of the top galleries in Sydney, while her knowledge of law has been a big blessing in her business dealings.

The Pain of Regret Is Greater
Than the Pain of Self-Discipline

They are able, because they think they are able.
— Virgil

- Every dream has its price and reward. When you're inspired by your purpose, you're willing to pay the price and accept the pain and pleasure of self-discipline.

- If you don't fill your life with what you do love, it becomes filled with what you don't.

- When you dedicate or commit your life to your purpose, your inner magnificence begins to unfold.

- Taking action steps of love cures years of fears, and bouts of doubts.

Many years ago, when I was in professional school, I saw an interview with a man celebrating his 103rd birthday. The reporter cheerfully asked him what he was going to wish for when he blew out his birthday candles. The man looked up at her with tears in his eyes and said, "I'm going to wish that I can come back here again with more courage, to do even more of the things I dreamed about but was afraid to try."

I still remember the look in that man's eyes. In some ways it's been an inspiration that has motivated me to stay on my mission and continue to do what I love and love what I do. The pain of regret truly is greater than that of self-discipline.

The Truth Is . . .

And I have the firm belief in this now,
not only in terms of my own experience,
but in knowing about the experience of others,
that when you follow your bliss,
doors will open where you would not have thought
there were going to be doors, and where there
wouldn't be a door for anybody else.
— Joseph Campbell

- Loving what you do helps you to do more of what you love.

- When you do what you love, you can prosper more effectively in all areas of your life.

- Your body knows when you're doing what you love and supports your mission with healing energy and vitality.

- Your life is most fulfilling when you pursue your primary purpose—the one you love.

- When you do what you love and love what you do, you're openhearted and thankful, and your heart and soul speak to you and guide you.

Reflections

Whatever you can do or dream, you can begin it.
— Johann Wolfgang von Goethe

1. Recall the last time you loved what you were doing so much that time passed without your noticing.

2. Take your memories back to childhood. Think about what you said you wanted to be when you grew up when you were in kindergarten, in the third grade, and in the sixth grade. Ask yourself if any of these dreams still stir your heart.

3. Ask yourself if you love what you do—be honest.

4. Take a few minutes to imagine what your life might be like if you were doing what you love.

Realizations

Live your dream.
— Athena Starwoman

1. If you knew you couldn't fail, what would you be, do, and have? Write this down in great detail.

2. Write ten things you like and ten things you dislike about your current position. Then write at least one way that each of these things is preparing you and helping you do what you love.

3. Write the first three action steps you would take to do what you love. Commit to doing the first step within the coming week.

4. Start a love list. Beginning today, when you see, hear, or experience something that brings a tear of gratitude to your eyes, write it down. Over time you'll begin to see a pattern emerge in your list, and this will help you clarify your primary purpose and motivate you to do what you love.

Affirmations

- *I do what I love, and I love what I do.*

- *The more I love what I do, the more I can do what I love.*

- *I take action steps in love to overcome my fear.*

- *I am prepared to accept the pain and the pleasures of doing what I love.*

- *When I am committed to my purpose, my body, mind, heart, and soul thrive and support me.*

- *My energy is infinite when I am inspired in love.*

- *I heal my body by doing what I am lovingly inspired to do.*

Chapter 4

As You Believe, So You Achieve

All that we are is the result of our thoughts.
— Buddha

What Are You Feeding Yourself?

We all know that healthy food nourishes and heals our bodies. But most people don't realize that healthy thoughts are food for the heart and soul. In fact, healthy, uplifting, and self-affirming thoughts actually help you to heal your body and achieve your life's goals! Thoughts of doubt and fear, however, block your belief in yourself and get in the way of your desired achievements.

Studies have shown that on the average, more than 50 percent of the thoughts people have are self-deprecatory. It's no wonder, then, that many people find it challenging to make healthy and inspiring changes in their lives, and more difficult still to achieve their dreams.

Thoughts are the mind's nutrition. When we focus

on our inspirations and concentrate our thinking in the direction of our desired objectives, we pave the way for great achievement. Altering our thoughts changes our lives because our consciousness attracts and perpetuates what we think about, and what we believe. If we focus on prosperity, we attract prosperity; and if we focus on poverty, we attract poverty. In other words, as we believe, so we achieve.

I began to learn this healing principle when I was 17 years old. At the time, I was living in Hawaii. It was there that I met a 93-year-old gentleman named Dr. Paul Bragg, who made a major difference in my life. One night he led a meditation that I'll never forget because that was when I first saw my vision of what I was going to do in this lifetime.

Dr. Bragg said, "I want you to decide what you want to commit your life to before we do the meditation, because whatever you come out of the meditation with is what you're going to do in life."

Well, when you're 17 years old, that's a big question! I remember thinking, *Do I really have to decide right now?* But when I asked myself the question a few times and considered the possibilities, the answer began to formulate. Now, at that time I was a high school dropout, living and surfing on the north shore of Oahu. I also had a health problem. So I put those observations together, then looked at my past. I didn't have much of an education. My first-grade teacher had told my parents and me that I'd probably never amount to much; that I wouldn't effectively read, write, or communicate. When I remembered her statement just then, it sparked an intense desire to beat the odds and begin learning again. So I put all of those factors together and decided that I wanted to dedicate my life to researching and discovering universal laws as they relate to body, mind, and soul—particularly as they applied to health.

When I went into that meditation, I saw myself speaking to large groups of people. I had no experience with public speaking, but that vision was so crystal clear and I was so present that I had tears of inspiration. When I came out of that meditation, I was overwhelmed by this vision. I thought, *Here I am, a high school dropout, and I'm going to travel around the world and share universal principles of healing—sure—that sounds like a neat idea. . . .* To make things even more interesting, at the time I was living in a tent with some other surfers.

During that summer, Dr. Bragg was giving lectures in the center of the island. Thinking that he'd be a good mentor, I hitchhiked in every morning to jog and have breakfast with him. One day I told him that I was overwhelmed and frightened by the vision I'd had during the meditation: "I don't see how I could possibly achieve that. It's so far away from where I am today."

With a big smile, he looked at me and said, "That's no problem, son. Is there anything else?"

I was taken aback for a second, but then replied, "Well, no, that's enough."

And Dr. Bragg said, "Okay, here's what you do. Just say this one phrase to yourself every day for the rest of your life, and don't miss a single day. Say to yourself, *I am a genius and I apply my wisdom,* and everything else will take care of itself."

So I hitchhiked back to the north shore, and all the way back I said to myself, *I'm a genius and I apply my wisdom.* And when I went into the tent I said, "Hey guys, I'm a genius and I apply my wisdom!"

They looked over their shoulders at me, laughed, and said, "Sure you are, John, whatever you say." Basically this was the first support group (ha ha) to encourage me in this vision. I continued to say this statement over and over again all day as I walked on the beach, as I surfed, and as I lay awake at night. Then, one evening while I was walking on the beach admiring the stars, I realized that I was experiencing a major shift in my thoughts, and I decided that I wanted to go home and share my vision with my parents. There I was encouraged to take a high school equivalence exam and earn my General Education Degree, which is the equivalent of a high school diploma. I passed! And soon I applied to, and found myself accepted by, Wharton College.

About a year and a half later, while I was sitting in the library studying mathematics, someone asked for help with a few problems. I began explaining how to work the first problem, and after a few minutes, more than a dozen people had gathered around the table, listening and asking questions. I was really getting into what I was doing when suddenly I heard this guy about three rows back from where I was sitting say, "That guy's a genius!" And I immediately flashed back to what Dr. Paul Bragg had said to me almost two years earlier. I realized at that moment what power this consistent affirmation has.

I later found out that a genius is someone who listens to the light of their soul and obeys. And wisdom is the light of the soul. I realized that what I had been affirming is that I commit my life to listening to my own heart and soul. Dr. Bragg actually was telling me to listen to that wisdom inside myself, tap in to it, experience it, take action steps in faith, do services of love, and follow what that inner whisper guides me to do. I continue to be amazed at how profound that guidance is, and at what a magnificent gift Dr. Bragg gave to me.

You Move in the Direction of Your Dominant Thoughts

Mental whispers develop dynamic power
to reshape matter into what you want . . .
Whatever you believe in intensely,
your mind will materialize.
— Paramahansa Yogananda

- To succeed in any undertaking whatsoever, it's vital that you concentrate on what you intend to do.

- Habits are thoughts applied over time to form predictable patterns in our physical, emotional, mental, or spiritual structures.

- Your consciousness attracts and perpetuates that which you think and believe.

- The more persistent a thought over time, the stronger its influence from minute to minute, day to day, and year to year.

Our minds are purified bit by bit as we learn to edit our dominant thoughts by dissolving the exaggerated or deprecating self-talk, and by amplifying the clear and loving messages of our hearts and souls. When we nourish our minds with inspirational reading, beautiful music, and empowering affirmations, we attract inspiration and beauty, and we're empowered.

When we focus our minds on fear and doubt, we sabotage our chances for achievement. When we focus our minds on our plans of action, we program ourselves for success.

Over the years, I've had the opportunity to meet with and consult numerous very successful people who achieve what they desire as a matter of course. I ask many of them to name the most important ingredient in their success. Most of them say that the thought of *not* succeeding doesn't occur to them. They simply believe they can do what they set out to do.

I've learned that we all have the ability to believe in ourselves and our ideas, but sometimes we haven't awakened it yet. A great example of this is the story of a man named Martin who wanted to open a computer store. He had a wise plan and enough money saved, with potential investors on standby, but he wasn't sure if he could really do it. He scheduled a half-day consultation with me, during which I explained the concept of achieving what we believe.

He was a little leery at first, saying that he wasn't sure if he really could overcome his fears. I suggested to him that he write a page of affirmations supporting his dream, and say them at least twice every day. I also suggested that he read the biographies of other successful people to fill his mind with inspired possibilities. Martin said that he was anxious to begin, and told me that he'd keep me posted.

Exactly 18 months later, Martin opened his doors for business. When he sent me an invitation to the store's grand opening, he wrote: "The more I read about the other people who succeeded, the more I could see myself achieving similar types of goals, and the most amazing thing is that I can see so clearly how my life shifted when my beliefs shifted." Today, Martin owns a chain of stores, his company is thriving, and he's well on his way to becoming a multimillionaire.

Achievement Starts with a Single Great Thought

We are what we think.
All that we are arises with our thoughts.
With our thoughts we make the world.
— The Dhammapada

- Everything in existence began as a thought.

- You have many great thoughts, you just have to silence your brain noise so you can hear them.

- Nobody knows how far a great thought or idea of today will travel, or who it will reach tomorrow.

- Inspired thoughts create inspired dreams.

Nearly all success stories begin with a single great thought that was nourished with belief. And many of the people with the greatest success stories faced some of the greatest adversity. When Walt Disney first applied to newspapers as a cartoonist, he was turned down flat. One editor even told him that he had no talent and should find something else to do with his life. But he had a thought that turned into a vision, and he persevered and continued to believe in himself.

About six years ago, a woman named Lauren attended

The Breakthrough Experience. She said that she'd been focused on having a successful and lucrative singing career, but once the ball started rolling toward big opportunities, she became frightened and began to worry that she might not have what it takes. As soon as she stopped believing in herself, the phone stopped ringing with offers to perform, and the same people who seemed anxious to talk with her a month earlier weren't returning her calls. She knew that her lack of belief was playing a major role in the shift her life had taken, and she wanted to get back to believing in herself but wasn't sure how.

During the two-day program, Lauren discovered that her lopsided perception of success was blocking her belief in her abilities. She said that she was infatuated with the idea of becoming a star, and she felt undeserving of so much success. I used The Demartini Method to help Lauren balance her perceptions and see that her success would bring an equal amount of pleasure and pain. Once she saw all the blessings and drawbacks in balance, her heart opened to her dream and she was filled with inspiration.

Lauren made a commitment to herself to stay focused on her goals and to support her vision with daily affirmations and visualizations of her achievement. Now she supports herself and her three children with her singing career. I recently received a postcard from her, mailed from Los Angeles, where she had traveled to record her first compact disc. She wrote: "The more I believe, the more I achieve."

The Truth Is . . .

Like attracts like.
Whatever the conscious mind thinks and believes,
the subconscious identically creates.
— Brian Adams

- You become your dominant thoughts.

- You alter your life by altering your thinking.

- If you have the idea, you have the ability to manifest it.

- Each thought is an opportunity to forge the first link in a new chain of habit.

- Unbalanced dominant thoughts produce an unappealing disharmony that results in brain noise.

- Balanced dominant thoughts produce unconditional love and set the stage for achievement.

Reflections

Whatever you vividly imagine,
ardently desire, sincerely believe,
and enthusiastically act upon,
must inevitably come to pass.
— Paul Meyer

1. What would you most like to achieve right now?

2. Close your eyes and visualize yourself as having already achieved whatever you think you'd most like to accomplish. Imagine this successful scenario in as much detail as you can, and make sure you place yourself in the picture!

3. Think of three times when your firm belief in a thought or idea resulted in a successful venture.

4. Begin editing your dominant thoughts. Dissolve the fears and the exaggerating and deprecatory self-talk. Affirm your ability to achieve.

Realizations

You are given the gifts of the gods;
you create your reality according to your beliefs.
Yours is the creative energy that makes the world.
There are no limitations to the self, except those you believe in.
— Jane Roberts

1. Conduct a personal experiment. Set your watch alarm or a timer to go off every 30 minutes throughout the day. Each time the alarm rings, jot down the exact thought you were having right before the alarm or timer sounded.

2. In order of importance to you, list the three highest-priority goals or objectives you wish to achieve.

3. Write seven affirmations for each of the three goals you listed.

4. Read the success stories of people whose achievements you admire.

Affirmations

*   *I am a genius, and I apply my wisdom.*

*   *As I believe, I achieve.*

*   *I am nourishing my heart and soul with healthy thoughts and inspirational books and tapes.*

*   *I am consciously focusing my dominant thoughts to support the dreams I would love to achieve.*

*   *If I can imagine it, I can achieve it.*

*   *I am seeing my body heal.*

Chapter 5

What You Sow, You Shall Reap

If you want to be loved, love and be lovable.
— Benjamin Franklin

Do You Know the Golden Rule?

Try as we might, it's impossible to break the Golden Rule. This supreme universal law of cause and effect encompasses all other truths. Whatever we put energy into—whether it's a thought, a word, or an action—eventually returns to us like a boomerang. Both the positive and the negative energies we send out into the world roll back like snowballs, picking up size and speed as they return.

If we sow love, we reap love. If we sow hate, we reap hate. It's such a simple concept that many people miss its deeply profound meaning. This principle is the reason we have the freedom to determine and choose what we'll reap or gain in our lives. If we want to receive life's rich blessings, it's up to us to earn them. Blessings don't come to us by way of luck, they're the results of our productivity and of our words or deeds to others.

This universal law has been illustrated throughout recorded history, and yet the first session with many of my clients is devoted to helping them understand that they're responsible for the effects in their lives.

I remember a man named Morty who complained that all day long his customers treated him impatiently and with very little respect. He was convinced that they acted this way because he was a carpet salesman. He didn't see how his own actions were sowing the seeds for the results he was getting. I asked Morty how he greeted customers when they came into his store. "Whaddaya mean, how do I greet 'em? I don't greet 'em. It's not the welcome wagon, it's a carpet store!"

"Well," I asked, "do you check on your customers to see if they need help while they're shopping?"

"Look, Doc, I don't think you're getting the gist of what I'm saying here. I run a carpet store. It's simple. They want carpet, and I got carpet! What's to help? I put tags on every piece of carpeting that give all the details and the price. People are supposed to come in, find what they want, tell me what it is, and pay for it," Morty explained.

"Morty," I asked, "do you know life's Golden Rule?"

His eyes went up, then down, and to the side, as if he were peering into his memory, and then he shrugged his shoulders and said, "Nope, sure don't."

I spent the next few hours helping Morty understand the Golden Rule and how it works. I explained that when he sent out thoughts of not wanting to be bothered, he planted the seeds for a harvest of customers who treated him with the same lack of respect he felt for them. I suggested that he begin greeting his customers and letting them know that he was there if they needed assistance. He was resistant to the idea, but agreed that he'd try it.

After one month of sowing a sincerely caring attitude for his customers, Morty called to tell me he was reaping respect and making record profits. "Now I know why you call it the Golden Rule!" he said. Then he added, "No—seriously—this stuff really works, and I've been saving money on aspirins and antacids, too. Thanks, Doc!"

Your Actions Determine Your Results

I shall never believe that God plays dice with the world.
— Albert Einstein

- Whatever you put energy into today, produces results tomorrow.

- When you think productive thoughts, you attract productive enterprises.

- When you respect and take care of your body, your body produces energy, strength, and health.

- Both "good luck" and "bad luck" are illusions. The universe is not a game of chance, it's a tangible demonstration of cause and effect.

The outcomes you experience in your life are ultimately neither "good" nor "bad." They're merely the predictable effects that result from whatever actions—or lack of actions—you've thought of and taken (or not). The universe doesn't judge; it balances. All compensations you've experienced in life are simply the sum of all the energies you've sent out in life. Everything you reap, whether you think it's a good thing or not, has just as many benefits as drawbacks and presents an opportunity for you to learn unconditional love for yourself and others. We know that our actions determine our results when it comes to short-term goals in life, like following instructions to put together a toy or an appliance, or mixing all of the required ingredients to bake a cake. But when it comes to long-term causes and effects, we often forget that this same principle holds true.

A few years ago, a man by the name of George came to The Breakthrough Experience in a wheelchair. He had no paralysis, but his knees were so stiffened by arthritis that it was extremely difficult for him to stand and exhausting for him to walk. He had just retired from an architecture firm where he'd worked for 30 years. He came to The Breakthrough Experience to decide what to do with the rest of his life. He said:

> I'm 62 years old, and by God I'm going to spend the rest of my life doing something that I want to do. No more dragging myself off to a job that I can't stand every day, designing cold office buildings that people hate to go to! I liked my job for the first 18 years, but then my supervisor transferred to another division and I never got used to the new guy or his ways. All Karl cares about is profit. The creative part of my job was completely eliminated, and after a while all the projects seemed the same. But I was determined to stick it out until my retirement! And I have to say I gave Karl a run for his money in the meantime. I was no pushover. I made him earn everything I gave him.

I asked George what he wanted to do now, and he said he wasn't sure. "When I was younger," he said, "before the arthritis got really bad, I thought I'd design and build dream houses. But now, I really don't know." I suggested that we begin The Demartini Method, and explained that it would help to clarify his perceptions. When we experience this truth, we're immersed in the unconditional love that our heart and soul is always revealing to us, but that we usually block with lopsided perceptions, emotions, and lies.

George decided that he wanted to complete The Demartini Method on Karl, the supervisor he didn't like. As George worked on the Method, he began to see that he himself had also done all the things he disliked Karl for doing. He also began to recognize a pattern that began at the time Karl was hired as his supervisor and continued up through the time his arthritis became more severe.

I shared with George that a stiffening of the knees is sometimes the body's way of expressing that we don't want to bend our knees and give in to authority. And I asked him how long he'd been describing his job as one he couldn't stand. Tears began to come to his eyes and he said, "For about as long as I've known Karl." I suggested that he keep working on The Demartini Method, until he reached a point where he could see Karl's magnificence and knew how Karl was a blessing and had served him in his life.

George was the last person in the program to complete his Method that night, but by the time he had, he could see that Karl simply gave back everything that George had dished out over the years. He saw clearly how his own actions determined the results. He was also able to see how his experience with Karl had helped him grow; how it made him more determined and gave him the courage to start over at the age of 62.

George also realized that he'd been programming his body with thoughts of "holding firm" in his position; "never bowing down" and "not being able to stand" his job. He also recognized the perfection of the many aspects of his relationship with Karl, and he thanked him for being the best teacher that he ever had. When he did, George's heart opened, tears of gratitude rolled down his cheeks, and a wave of unconditional love swelled in the hearts of everyone present. There wasn't a dry eye in the room when George stood up and walked around the conference table to hug and thank a participant who reminded him—and played out the role—of Karl.

The next day George came to the program without his wheelchair. He was still stiff, but he was walking! He proudly announced that he'd be available to design and build a dream house for anyone who was interested.

Plant Flowers or Forever Pull Weeds

The beginning is the most important part of the work.
— Plato

- When we don't plant flowers, we forever pull weeds.

- Once you plant the flowers, don't let the weeds take over.

- Every time a weed is pulled, the flowers become more visible.

- Whatever we don't love in life becomes our weeds.

But in all fairness, one person's weeds are another's flowers! When I was a little boy growing up in a suburb of Houston, I lived next door to an elderly woman named Mrs. Grubs. Her beautifully landscaped yard was filled with colorful flowers. Hummingbirds and honeybees daily visited the fragrant honeysuckle blossoms. She was a master of gardening, and I enjoyed helping her water her plants.

At that time, my parents' house was surrounded by grass, which was constantly growing up alongside the house, and I was constantly pulling it out. By the time I'd gotten it all pulled on one side of the house and worked my way around to the other side, I'd have to start all over again. It seemed so futile.

One hot day, when I was outside pulling the tall grass and weeds, Mrs. Grubs happened to be in her yard and saw how frustrated I was with my work. She walked over to the fence between the houses and, leaning on her side of the fence, stated something so profound that I can still hear it today. She said to me, "John, if you don't plant flowers in your garden, you'll forever be pulling weeds." At that age, I learned the lesson literally, but as I grew older and Mrs. Grubs's words lingered in my mind, I began to see how they applied to every aspect of my life.

The Truth Is . . .

If you want to lift yourself up, lift up someone else.
— Booker T. Washington

- It's impossible to break the Golden Rule of cause and effect; no matter what, you reap what you sow.

- Blessings have nothing to do with so-called luck. They result from your thoughts, words, and actions.

- Whether initially you see it as a benefit or a drawback, everything you reap serves you and provides you with an opportunity to sow unconditional love.

- Your health and well-being tomorrow is the result of what you do, think, and believe today.

Reflections

A man's deeds are his life.
— West African saying

1. Review your day and look for the link between what you sowed and what you reaped.

2. Review your day again, only this time visualize yourself sowing the seeds of what you'd love to reap, and see yourself reaping those loves.

3. Think of a situation in your life that somehow improved when you pulled the weeds surrounding it.

4. Identify an area in your life that would prosper if you "planted flowers," then commit to sowing whatever you'd most love.

Realizations

Work is love made visible.
— Kahlil Gibran

1. List three situations in your life that you perceive as negative.

2. Select one of the situations above that you'd most like to see in a balanced perspective, and write 30 things about that situation that you dislike or see as negative. Now review your list and, for each of the 30 aspects you perceive as negative, recall a time in your life when you did the same thing or its equivalent. Be honest, and look carefully.

3. Go back over your list once again. This time write down at least one way each aspect you perceived as negative has benefited or served you. (You may want to set this up in three columns, as in the following example.)

Situation I'd Like to See in Balance: My Marriage		
Things I Dislike	What I've Done	How It Serves Me
My husband ignores me	I've ignored my son	New hobbies
Ironing my family's clothes	My mom ironed mine	Time to daydream

4. Write a thank-you letter to the universe, expressing gratitude for the opportunities that your situation has provided you to sow and reap unconditional love.

Affirmations

*   *I am sowing what I love to reap.*

*   *I am planting flowers and pulling weeds in my life's gardens. I plant seeds of production and harvest profitable results.*

*   *I respect my role as creator of my life and I am grateful that my actions determine my results.*

*   *I sow healthy thoughts to reap health.*

Chapter 6

Every Loving Wish Is Possible

*Every moment of your life is infinitely creative
and the universe is endlessly bountiful.
Just put forth a clear enough request and
everything your heart desires must come to you.*
— Shakti Gawain

How Much Are Your Wishes Worth?

Every loving wish is possible, including the wish for balanced health. But we need to invest more than a few coins in a fountain if we want to make our inspired dreams and wishes come true. The reality is that we're meant to devote ourselves to our inspirations. That's precisely our purpose in life. But for some reason, we don't always believe that we deserve to live our dreams, so instead of reaching for the stars, which is our destiny, we cling to our illusions and settle for mediocrity.

But we don't have to settle for anything less than what we would love! We have everything that we need to succeed in the pursuit of our heartfelt dreams, no matter what they are. Only illusory fears stand in our way, and actions with gratitude dissolve fear as light permeates darkness. In fact, when we're truly grateful for all that we are and all that we have, our hearts and souls guide us in the direction of our most loving wishes and our most inspired purpose.

A few months ago, I received a package from a woman named Rosalyn, whom I had never met. In the package was a birth announcement, a photograph of a baby boy, and a thank-you letter, which read:

Dear Dr. Demartini,

My husband Bruce and I want to thank you for the part you played in the birth of Christopher, our miracle baby. We wanted a baby with all our heart, but according to our doctor we had a near-zero percent chance of conceiving without fertility drugs. I didn't want to take the drugs, and my biological clock was about to strike 45.

My 45th birthday was on a Friday, so I decided to take a vacation day and enjoy a three-day weekend. Bruce surprised me with breakfast in bed, and I decided to see what was on television while I was eating. As I was flipping through the channels, you caught my attention. You were a guest on a health show and were telling a woman in the audience that "every loving wish is possible." As I listened, I realized that the woman was experiencing problems with infertility—just like me. Her story was so similar to my own that I felt a lump in my throat and began to cry. I felt like you were talking directly to me when you told her to count her blessings every morning and every night and not to stop until she felt her heart open to the unconditional love and guidance of her soul. And you said, "When you are grateful for what you have, you attract more blessings into your life."

Well, I took your advice and so did my husband, and three months later I found out I was pregnant. Christopher

*is one month old, very healthy, and a bigger blessing than
we ever dreamed he would be.*

    Thank you,

    Rosalyn, Bruce, and Christopher

Every Miracle Starts as a Dream

There is nothing like a dream to create the future.
— Victor Hugo

- Dreams represent your ultimate values. They're the playground of your mind, where every loving wish is possible.

- Inspired dreams are the driving force of all great acts and deeds.

- A dream is a magic vine that you can climb to a new plane of awareness; where you can practice your words, perform your actions, imagine your calculations, design your monuments, and explore the farthest reaches of imagination.

- All that you can conceive, you can achieve.

A miracle is merely an event that doesn't follow the scientific theories of the day. For example, scientific tests said that Rosalyn couldn't conceive, but Rosalyn said otherwise! Science is a magnificent process, but it's light-years away from having all the answers to the puzzles of our complex universe. So when it comes to matters of the heart, it's wiser to listen to your inner guiding voice than heed the limitations that are expressed by some scientists who doubt and other unbelieving people.

When you listen to the wisdom of your heart and soul—and obey—you live a life of unconditional love, which is ripe for miracles of every type imaginable. Unconditional love heals your body and mind and energizes your dreams and inspirations.

About ten years ago, I was blessed with the opportunity to meet a miracle worker named Joe, a custodian who worked miracles in the lives of the children who attended the school he took pride in cleaning. It was a small school with an even smaller operating budget, but Joe loved his job, and he really loved the children. He knew many of their names and spoke to them with respect and in a friendly manner.

He paid particular attention to those children he could see were struggling. In that low-income neighborhood, some of the children came to school day after day without a lunch. On some days, Joe made more than 20 sandwiches, which he placed in the children's desks when they went outside for morning recess. When he had time, he put stickers on the wrapping and signed them "from one of your angels."

One summer afternoon, I ran into Joe in the city park. He was radiating energy, and I asked him what he'd been doing during his summer vacation. "Actually," he said, "I've been volunteering my time at the school. We're building a small addition for a cafeteria and lunchroom for the kids. And the school got some government funding so the kids who can't afford it don't need to pay."

I asked Joe how the school district raised the money to build the addition, and he humbly admitted that he'd been running a campaign for the past several years. He said, "I knew the pain of hunger when I was a child, and it's been a lifelong wish and dream for me to help feed hungry children." He told me that when he first began raising funds for the project, a lot of people thought he was only kidding himself, but he believed in his dream, and the donations kept rolling in!

You're Destined to Make Your Inspired Dreams Come True

Go confidently in the direction of your dreams!
Live the life you've imagined.
— Henry David Thoreau

- You have what you need to make your inspired dream come true.

- Your dreams are your visions and your callings.

- To fulfill your dreams, you must be willing to sacrifice your illusions.

- When you follow your inspired dreams, you attract into your life the people, places, things, ideas, and events that can make your loving wishes possible.

Your inspired dreams are the lifeblood of your heart and soul. They're your reason for being. When you follow this inner guide and pursue your dreams, you're destined to succeed. By obeying the wisdom of your heart and soul and taking definite action, you transform your dreams into tangible reality.

A year or so ago, a woman named Linda attended one of my personal success programs called Prophecy. When she arrived, she told me that she had an inspired vision of what she would love do, but when she looked at everything logically, her dream seemed to be beyond impossible.

I explained to Linda that if she focused on her dream in detail, and took action steps guided by her inspirations, she would literally attract into her life the people, events, and resources she needed to fulfill the dream. Later in the week, she shared that her dream was to start what she called a "house-nanny" service. She knew that many nanny services provided capable men and women to take care of children. Her vision was to create a service that provided efficient and resourceful men and women to take care of the household, for the parents who wanted to take care of their children themselves.

Many of the other program participants thought it was a great idea, and as the week went on, Linda began to see how she could begin taking action steps to make her dream business a reality. In fact, she was so focused on the concept that by the end of the seven-day program she had placed an ad in the newspaper to find people to fill house-nanny positions, and two program participants gave her the names of couples they knew who would be interested in the house-nanny service.

The Truth Is . . .

All that we see or seem
Is but a dream within a dream.
— Edgar Allan Poe

- When you follow your inspired dreams, you obtain light, love, wisdom, and power.

- As the master of your dreams, you have the will to obey the wisdom of your heart and soul.

- Your heart and soul speak the language of unconditional love and gratitude.

- Every loving wish is possible, because every inspired desire has a destiny to come true.

Reflections

Set your sights high, the higher the better.
Expect the most wonderful things to happen,
not in the future but right now.
— Eileen Caddy

1. Think of three wishes you've made when tossing coins into a fountain or blowing out your birthday candles that have come true.

2. Take a moment to think about each of the wishes you've recalled and ask yourself if any of these desires were inspired or heartfelt.

3. Think of at least two people you know who believe in their dreams and are pursuing them. Invite them to lunch as your mentors.

4. Take five minutes right now to close your eyes and let your inspired dreams take you away.

Realizations

Ask, and it shall be given you; seek, and ye shall find; knock, and it shall be opened unto you.
— Matthew 7:7

1. Recall one or two instances in your life when other people tried to discourage you from pursuing a goal, but you kept your sights on your objective and succeeded by doing so.

2. Of the instances you recalled, select the one for which you feel most grateful and write a detailed description of that occasion. Make sure you include your inspirational guidance, your feelings of love, and your actions.

3. Sit in a comfortable chair and begin to count your blessings. Think of everything and everyone for whom you feel true gratitude. Keep your mind and thoughts focused on your moments of gratefulness until your eyes fill with tears of inspiration. Then ask your inner voice to reveal an inspired dream to you.

4. Take the first action step toward pursuing the inspired dream that was revealed.

Affirmations

- *I open my heart with gratitude to hear the wisdom of my soul.*

- *I have the wisdom and discipline to listen to the guidance of my heart and soul—and obey.*

- *Every one of my loving and healing wishes is possible.*

- *I am grateful for my dreams and inspirations.*

Chapter 7

If You Don't Know Where You're Going, You'll End Up Somewhere Else

The biggest temptation is to settle for too little.
— Thomas Merton

Are You Navigating Without a Clear Direction?

Your best chance of ending up where you want to be is to know precisely where you're going. And that applies to healing your body as well as it applies to everything else you do. But while many people know this intuitively, few people actually practice it in their daily lives. I've seen a number of people carefully plan their 2 or 3 weeks of annual vacation, but fail to plan the other 49 or 50 weeks of the year. So instead of being guided by their own plans, they often flounder for lack of a clear direction or purpose.

Many people schedule consultations with me because they're not experiencing the fulfillment they wish to have in their lives. They're often bored with their career and feel as though their lives have no real meaning. Many of them say that they don't know what they want to be doing, but they're certain it isn't what they're doing now. The interesting thing is that after a bit of discussion, I generally discover that they do, in fact, know what they'd love to do. What they don't know is that they can do it. People often disregard their most inspired ideas and settle for whatever seems reasonable, or whatever comes their way.

Those who are the most energized and on track, however, are the ones who are heading toward an inspired destination, and working toward a defined purpose. These men and women organize their lives in the direction of their heartfelt inspirations. Consequently, everything takes on more meaning and becomes more fulfilling.

Gene was 43 when he first began consulting with me. He was working as a landscape architect at a major university, making a significant amount of money, and feeling incredibly uninspired about his job and his life. He felt that his life was half over and said he still had no idea what he really wanted to do. However, as we talked, I sensed that Gene did have a hidden dream but for some reason was dismissing it.

I asked him a number of questions about his hobbies and the things he enjoyed doing in his free time, and a pattern began to emerge. Gene loved the outdoors! He chose to pursue a career in landscape architecture because he thought it would provide him with lots of opportunities to work outside. Instead, for the previous ten years he'd spent the majority of his time in an office, wearing a tie, pushing paper, and delegating outdoor projects to his staff.

"When I was younger, I thought it would be cool to be a forest ranger and get paid to hike in the woods and groom trails and take care of the park. But I could never take a pay cut like that now," he said. "None of the outdoor jobs that I'd like can pay me enough to support my family. So I'm really just looking for something different that's at least a little better than what I'm doing now."

Gene was stuck in the illusion that in order to make the same amount of money, or more, he had to settle for a career that was less fulfilling than one he really wanted. In fact, he was so certain of this belief that he hadn't done any research to investigate other career choices that would offer the income he desired. He also hadn't considered the possibility of creating a position for himself by offering his expertise and knowledge to corporations, forestry divisions, and private land owners. I suggested to Gene that he devote at least ten solid hours to researching future career possibilities about which he truly felt inspired.

A few weeks later, Gene practically burst into my office in a swirl of energy to tell me that he knew what he would love to do. "I'm going to be a land-management consultant," he said. Having discovered that he already had enough contacts to begin his consulting business part-time, evenings and weekends, Gene estimated that it would take three to five years before he'd be completely on his own.

But only two years after Gene and I had this meeting, he was earning more than $80,000 a year in his consulting business—far more than his university position had paid. "Once I knew exactly where I'd love to go, and you were sure I could find a way to get there, I realized that I really could do it!" he said. Gene was inspired by knowing that he could turn his avocation into his vocation.

I recently received some beautiful photographs that Gene took while consulting near Grand Canyon National Park. His note read: "The past five years have been the most fulfilling years of my life. I love what I'm doing, I appreciate my skills more, I enjoy my family more, and all around my life has more meaning and energy."

Follow the Dream in Your Heart

> Trust your heart . . . never deny it a hearing.
> It is the kind of house oracle that often
> foretells the most important.
> — Baltasar Gracián y Morales

- You already know the essence of the dream in your heart, but you may not know that you know it.

- When you find yourself wavering and wandering, it's a sign that you've tuned out the wise guidance from your heart and soul.

- Your motivation miraculously increases once you begin to follow the dream in your heart.

- There is no substitute for action. Begin now.

Following the dream in your heart is like following the yellow-brick road to Oz. You're bound to meet adversity along the way, maybe even a wicked witch or two, but you'll face challenges like these no matter which road you take. And since no matter what you do, you're guaranteed to experience both pain and pleasure in your life, you might as well choose the path that offers the most fulfillment and ultimately the most enlightenment.

I recently had the pleasure of meeting a very articulate six-year-old girl named Emily during lunch at one of my favorite restaurants in Houston. She approached me and said, "You're Dr. Demartini." When I responded positively, she said, "I'm Emily. I'm from Tennessee."

At that moment, I made eye contact with a woman at a nearby table who'd been a chiropractic patient of mine more than six years earlier. She began to apologize for her daughter's interruption, but before she could, Emily hopped into the chair across from me and said, "My mom told me how you healed her back and then she was healthy enough to pick me up and play with me!"

By now her mother, Melissa, had also approached the table. "I didn't want to interrupt you," she said, "but since Emily already took care of that, do you have a minute?"

I invited them to join me for lunch, and Melissa began recounting the chain of events that had occurred since her recovery from her back problems: "For my entire life, I'd wanted to be a school teacher but, as you know, I'd had back problems since I was a child and could only stand up for about ten minutes at a time without experiencing pain. So I became a secretary, and then I became an accounting assistant, and then I became a stenographer. I was convinced that I couldn't be a teacher, so I kept trying to find other jobs that I could tolerate."

I remembered that when Melissa was a patient, she had just given birth to Emily. At that time, she said that she always just accepted her back problems as a part of her life. But now that she had Emily, she had a deep desire to heal her back so that she could do more with her daughter. Melissa continued: "You were the first doctor I ever met who believed that my back could be healed, and believed that I could be strong enough to do whatever I loved to do. Because of your certainty, I started to daydream about having a strong enough back to be able to play with Emily, and I began to think that maybe I could be a teacher someday! I found a new strength within myself and a new determination to heal and to teach."

I told her that I was pleased to see her doing so well, and I asked her what brought her back to Houston. "Well," she said proudly, "Thanks to you, I'm here to attend a teachers' conference!"

Focus on Your Primary Aim

Never look down to test the ground
before taking your next step;
only he who keeps his eyes fixed on the
far horizon will find the right road.
— Dag Hammarskjold

- Affirmations put you in line with what you're about to do.

- Steadiness, poise, serenity, and inner peace are signs that you're progressing.

- Keep your eyes on your primary aim, not just on the road immediately ahead.

- Roadblocks and obstacles are opportunities to learn unconditional love and to heal the wounds created by your illusions.

The more you focus on your purpose or your primary aim in life, the more you attract the people, places, situations, and resources that can help you on your journey. In fact, staying focused on your primary aim, or ultimate purpose, is the most effective way to get there. You may be tempted to put more energy into the obstacles and diversions on your path than you put into your heartfelt mission. But if you do, attending to these obstacles and diversions, along with their temptations, could become a habit. This may lead you, sooner or later, to decide falsely that you can't follow your dream.

You don't need to fall prey to this illusion! A tightrope walker is a great example of someone who keeps his or her eyes on their primary aim rather than just on the road ahead. When I was eight years old, I was amazed to see a boy about my age cross a tightrope in the circus. Later that day while waiting in line for an ice cream cone, I recognized the tightrope walker standing in line behind me. I asked him, "How can you cross that rope without ever looking at it?"

"That's the only way I can cross it!" he said. "I have to keep my eyes straight on the other platform or I fall off every time!"

After we got our ice cream he said, "Come over to this curb and I'll show you what I mean." For the next few minutes, I practiced walking on the curb. When I kept my eyes on the stop sign at the end of the curb, I kept my balance. But when I looked down at the curb, or when I looked at a piece of the curb that was ahead of me, I fell off. Although I've never seen the tightrope walker again, he was one of my wisest teachers, and the lesson he taught has helped me throughout my life.

The Truth Is . . .

An obstacle is something you see
when you take your eyes off the goal.
— Anonymous

- When you know where you're going, and you follow your heart and soul's guidance, you're certain to have a more fulfilling journey.

- When you're not focused on your primary purpose, the winds of change and indecision can toss you about like a rowboat in a storm.

- When you follow the dream in your heart, you're energized, inspired, and motivated.

- When you focus on your primary aim in life, you jump hurdles with ease.

- When you focus on your healing, you heal.

- When you follow the path of your inspirations, your body is strengthened, your mind is sharpened, and you're immersed in the healing power of unconditional love.

Reflections

We succeed only as we identify in life, or in war,
or in anything else, a single overriding objective,
and make all other considerations bend to that one objective.
— Dwight D. Eisenhower

1. Take a few moments to look at your life and determine if you're on the path you wish to be.

2. If you're on the path you desire, close your eyes and spend the next ten minutes focusing on your inspired purpose or direction. If you're not on that path, close your eyes and imagine yourself doing the activities about which you feel the most inspired.

3. Recall a time when your creativity or resourcefulness helped you clear, or go around, one of life's roadblocks. Acknowledge yourself for your ability to persevere.

4. Recall a time when keeping your eyes on your primary aim helped you stay on the path and maintain your balance.

Realizations

Be at peace and see a clear pattern
and plan running through all your lives.
Nothing is by chance.
— Eileen Caddy

1. Look into your future and write down what you would love to be, what you would love to do, and what you would love to have.

2. Clarify your highest lifetime priorities by writing your own obituary. Assume that you'll live to be at least 100 years old.

3. Take from three to five minutes to be thankful for your inspirations. Ask that any guidance you need come to you at the right time, and believe that it will.

4. Fill up a photo album with pictures that represent your answers to questions 1 and 2. They may be your own photos, pictures cut out of magazines, or sketches that you draw. The idea is to create a visual representation of your inspired dreams that will support your verbal affirmations with visual details.

Affirmations

- *I have the wisdom to follow the dream in my heart.*

- *I am focused on my purpose and destined to fulfill this focus.*

- *I am grateful for the opportunities offered by hurdles and inspired and poised to leap over them.*

- *I am using the infinite power of unconditional love to strengthen and heal my body in order to fulfill my inspired dreams.*

Chapter 8

Your Limitations Are All in Your Head

Do the thing, and you will have the power.
— Ralph Waldo Emerson

Are You in Your Own Way?

Many people have a long list of reasons to explain why they're not doing what they love, but few of them objectively examine their reasons and look for underlying fears. The reality is that there's a hidden fear behind every imagined limitation, including sickness. As much as we may be tempted to blame other people or outside circumstances for our current condition in life, sooner or later we realize that we attract and create our own limitations. And while that may be a humbling reality, it's also an inspiring one.

Since we attract or create our own limitations, we can also break through them—not by repressing, ignoring, or denying them, but by learning to love them. Yes! *Love them.* Because anything we don't love runs us and inhibits our inspired actions with fear. Our limitations represent all the aspects of ourselves and others that we haven't learned to love and appreciate yet. So each time we take an honest look at a limit or a block, we give ourselves an opportunity to love and to reach a higher level of awareness.

Every one of us has the creativity and ability necessary to rise above our own limitations. But sometimes the limitations feel comfortable, and the idea of achieving our dreams frightens us, and that's when we're most tempted to sabotage our own efforts. That's the frame of mind in which I found a young man named Jeremy when we met on an airplane.

I was working on my laptop computer when Jeremy sat down beside me and introduced himself. When he asked what I was working on, I told him that I was writing a book about the mind, body, heart, and soul connection, and the healing properties of inspiration and unconditional love. He nodded his head, but his eyes glazed over, and for the next half hour he was silent.

It wasn't until the flight attendant brought our meals that he said, "You know, I can't believe I'm sitting here next to someone who's writing a book. Do you know how long I've been wanting to write a book? How can I get from wanting to write a book, and talking about writing a book, to actually writing one?"

I explained to Jeremy that the only difference between wanting to write a book and actually writing one was taking action steps. "When I begin on a book," I said, "I know that it's a process, and I know that the book will change as the process continues."

Jeremy's eyes widened. "So you just do it. You just write one page at a time, and you like some stuff and you don't like other stuff and you change things, but you just keep writing until you have the book that you want!"

"Yes," I said, "that about sums it up."

Jeremy shook his head, smiling. "You have no idea how much what you just said means to me! For years I've been afraid to type a single word on my computer as if it's somehow getting chipped into stone or something. Writing a book is like doing anything else! It doesn't have to be perfect from the start; nothing is. Everything I do is a process . . . wow!"

I haven't run into Jeremy again since that conversation, but I'm sure that he's much closer to writing his book than he was before he realized that he was creating his own limitations.

Whatever You Feel Uncomfortable about— and Don't Love—Is Stopping You

Feel the fear; but don't let it stop you.
— Anonymous

- When you permit something about which you feel uncomfortable to stop you from pursuing your inspired dreams, you continue to attract its lessons into your life, until you face it and learn to love it.

- When you learn to love what you perceive to be a roadblock, you feel grateful for the lesson and the experience it presents.

- When you permit your discomforts to balloon into fears, you lose sight of your goal and see only the blocks in your path.

- When you permit fear to make decisions for you, your self-worth plummets.

Since you're human, you're guaranteed to experience discomfort. In fact, feeling uncomfortable is a wonderful gift. It tells you with certainty about an area or situation in your life that you have yet to learn to love. When you learn to love the blocks and messages of sickness that appear to be in your path, you conquer your own fears and move forward in your life. You can look at your worries and discomforts as the rungs on a ladder that leads to your inspired dream. Each time you grasp the next rung, you learn to love something new, and you're one step closer to your goal!

When I was in California teaching Prophecy, one of my personal success programs, I had the pleasure of meeting an extremely talented man named Lee. He enrolled in Prophecy to clarify his vision for life and to gain a better understanding of himself. Lee worked in the motion-picture business, but what he really wanted to do was start his own photography studio. "I've had this dream for more than ten years," he said, "but I haven't done anything more than think about it."

I helped Lee identify his fears and anxieties about starting his own business, and before long he was able to see a pattern of two dominant fears in his life. He said, "I don't like talking to people that I don't know, and I really don't like promoting my own work."

I knew that Lee was exaggerating the drawbacks and minimizing the benefits of talking with new people and marketing himself. I asked him to list 70 benefits and 70 drawbacks for both of his fears. At first he tried to dodge this balancing exercise: "I can tell you right now that there's nowhere near 70 benefits for either of those things!" I suggested that the other program participants begin collectively working on Lee's first fear—talking with people he didn't know. Within five minutes, 20 benefits were listed on the board, and Lee agreed to finish the exercise on his own.

"This is unbelievable! Now that I'm on a roll with the benefits, I'm actually having more trouble filling in the drawback columns!" Lee told me when I checked on his progress. He was beginning to see very clearly that he'd blown his own fears out of proportion and had been putting more faith in his anxiety than he was putting in himself. By the time he finished the exercise, he was actually laughing aloud at some of the things he had written. "I can't believe that I put off what I really want to do with my life for so long because I thought I had to overcome my fears first!" he said. "Now I can see that there really isn't all that much to be afraid of."

Today, Lee's photography studio is a successful business, and in addition to doing his own promotions, he now has two other marketing people working for him as well.

Self-Worth Is a State of Mind

What a man thinks of himself, that it is which
determines, or rather, indicates, his fate.
— Henry David Thoreau

- You can't be lifted up by anyone or anything any higher than you're willing to lift yourself up.

- You can't be put down by anyone or anything any lower than you're willing to put yourself down.

- No one will lift you up any higher than yourself.

- No one will put you down any lower than yourself.

When people praise and reprimand you, they're only providing you with their opinion and perceptions of your actions. Only if they reflect your own opinions can other people's opinions have the power to make you feel good or bad. You decide how you feel and your feelings are based on your values.

For example, in many countries, when invited to dinner, it's considered good to arrive on time, so being on time would be praised. But in other countries, it's more polite to be fashionably late, so arriving on time might be considered bad and would be reprimanded. The truth is, however, that being on time or late is neither good nor bad. It's just being on time or late. It only becomes good or bad if it becomes labeled that way. So seeking praise and avoiding reprimands from others can become one big game of distraction.

Many people go through life trying to receive praise and avoid reprimand. To them, other people's opinions define their own self-worth. But those who live their lives listening to the guidance of their hearts and souls realize that they must be true to themselves regardless of others' opinions of them.

True self-worth stems from within, and when you're focused on an inspired purpose, neither praise nor reprimand can bump you off your course. Mother Teresa is an example of a centered person who stayed on course whether she received praise or grief in return. She had the power to raise amazing sums of money for the causes she supported because she was inspired. Her own discomforts weren't permitted to stand in the way of her mission. She didn't acknowledge rejection. She walked in the certainty that her prayers would be answered—and so they were.

About two years ago, a woman named Brenda attended The Breakthrough Experience. She was having a difficult time with her boss and had been trying to find a new job for nearly a year. When I asked her what type of job she was looking for, she replied, "I don't care. I'll take whatever I can get. I just have to get away from my boss. She's ruining my life. I feel rotten at the end of every day." Then she added, "But I can't even get a job interview. I feel like I'm not good enough to compete with all those other people, and the more I get rejected, the less I want to fill out another job application."

Brenda was experiencing a low sense of self-worth. She was buying into other people's opinions instead of believing in herself. I explained to Brenda that self-worth is a state of mind. She could choose to accept the opinions of others, or she could look inside herself and find the truth.

That evening, after the program participants completed The Demartini Method, Brenda realized that her low self-worth had begun when she was a small child:

> When I was a little girl, I wanted so much to please my father, but no matter what I did, he would always tell me that I could do better. Well, when I was working

on The Demartini Method, I discovered that I'm doing the same thing to my own children. Just last week my daughter Andrea came home from school with four A's and two B's on her report card. And I just realized that instead of congratulating her, I said, "I knew you could do it, and I bet if you try a little harder, you can make all A's!"

When Brenda saw how similar her words to her daughter had been to those her father had said to her, she understood that her feelings of not being good enough stemmed from her childhood perception of what her father's words meant. "When I saw Andrea's grades," she said, "I felt pride in my heart, and I wanted her to know that I believed in her ability completely. And now I can see that my dad was feeling pride for me and believing in me, too."

The Truth Is . . .

Everything that enlarges the sphere of human powers,
that shows man he can do what he thought
he could not do, is valuable.
— Samuel Johnson

- By being truly humble and honest with yourself, you unveil your true potential and express your greatest self-worth.

- When you do what you love and love what you do, you experience the feeling of true worth and magnetically attract the people, places, things, ideas, and events that can help you fulfill your purpose in life.

- Your true worth is directly proportional to your gratitude for—and unconditional love of—life.

- What you feel thankful for heals.

Reflections

No noble thing can be done without risks.
— Michel Eyquen de Montaigne

1. Think of an occasion when you sabotaged your own efforts because you felt uncomfortable about taking the next step.

2. Think of an occasion when you felt uncomfortable about your next step, but took it anyway. Recall the feeling of achievement you experienced.

3. Close your eyes and visualize yourself taking a comfortable action step toward your inspired dream, about which you currently feel uncomfortable.

4. What you feel thankful for grows. Take a moment to be thankful for the self-worth you already possess.

Realizations

You miss 100 percent of the shots you never take.
— Wayne Gretzky

1. Write the steps that you want to take toward one of your goals but feel uncomfortable taking.

2. Circle the step that makes you the most uncomfortable or that creates the greatest fear or anxiety.

3. Make a commitment to begin doing whichever step you circled within the next seven days. Schedule it on your calendar and treat it as you would treat a commitment you make to a friend.

4. Plan something special for yourself as a celebration for keeping your commitment and take the next step toward your goal.

Affirmations

- *I am grateful for everything I am, do, and have.*

- *I am grateful for everything that comes my way.*

- *I am willing to accept the benefits and the drawbacks of moving toward my goals.*

- *I am as worthy as I believe I am, and no one can put me down or lift me up any more than I put myself down or lift myself up.*

- *I am experiencing the healing power of unconditional love, which has no limitations and no restrictions.*

Chapter 9

The Clearer Your Ultimate Purpose, the More Effectively You'll Fulfill It

When you are inspired by some great purpose, some extraordinary project, all your thoughts break their bonds, your mind transcends limitations, your consciousness expands in every direction, and you find yourself in a new, great, and wonderful world. Dormant forces, faculties, and talents become alive, and you discover yourself to be a greater person by far than you ever dreamed yourself to be.
— Patanjali

What Are You Doing Here?

From the beginning of recorded history, people have been asking questions like, *Why am I here?* and *What am I supposed to be doing?* You can look outside yourself for those answers—many people do—but the most inspiring answers come from within. When you listen to your inner voice, you can hear your life's calling or inspired purpose.

Once you begin fulfilling this purpose, you experience a new level of unconditional love and gratitude and a greater level of health, and you're inspired to achieve and accomplish dreams that might once have seemed impossible.

Historically, those who have listened to their inner voice and followed their inner vision have had the greatest impact on the world. Men and women like Joan of Arc, Galileo, Isaac Newton, Marie Curie, Susan B. Anthony, and Albert Einstein all followed an inner calling and vision. These inspired people pursued their ultimate purposes and, in return, experienced fulfillment and made lasting contributions to our lives. When we devote our own lives to our inspired calling, we have an immortal effect on the world.

You may not have heard your inspired purpose or inner calling yet, but I assure you that an enlightening purpose lives inside your heart and soul—one so profound that you'd be overwhelmed by its brilliance and magnificence if it were fully realized all at once. The inner urge you feel to question the meaning of your life compels you to discover your purpose and endeavor to fulfill it. The clearer and more definite your purpose, the more you become aligned with the infinite power and resources of the universe.

When you focus on a clear and definite purpose, your heart and soul guide you to take wise action steps and motivate you with unconditional love. When you think about your purpose and take steps toward its fulfillment, you rise to a higher level of understanding and you experience more love and gratitude for yourself, others, and the world. The more you focus on your life's mission, the more meaningful your life becomes.

Without a clear purpose, a person can swing back and forth, like a giant pendulum, from one extreme to the other in their thoughts, emotions, actions, and inactions. That's one of the reasons I was so inspired to create The Breakthrough Experience. I was blessed to be living an inspired life of purpose, and I wanted to share with other people what I'd learned and experienced.

A young man named Greg attended The Breakthrough Experience nearly seven years ago. At the time, he was single, 43 years old, worked in a manufacturing plant, and was very depressed. He said that for years he'd been asking, *Is this all there is?* "Part of me really thinks this is all there is, but then another part of me—sort of in the back of my mind—says there's more. I guess I'm here to find out."

As the program progressed, Greg shared that he loved to play the piano. There was a piano in the hallway outside our meeting room, and when we took our lunch break, Greg played a difficult work for the keyboard by Bach. He was very talented, but it was his love for the music and his inspired spirit that separated him from many of the other pianists whom I've heard play. Greg was truly one of the most inspired pianists I've had the privilege to hear and enjoy.

Later in the program when Greg was working on his purpose statement, he looked up with tears in his eyes and said, "My hand is shaking. I can't believe how hard it is for me to write this." I suggested to Greg that he look inside his heart and ask himself what he really felt called to do. He looked at me, then down at his hands, and said, "I always thought music could only be a hobby, but now I can see it's a gift that I'm supposed to share." As soon as he allowed himself to say those words, his inspired purpose began to crystallize in his mind and his heart.

Greg left that weekend with a clear focus and definite action steps to begin fulfilling his inspired purpose.

Since that time, he has performed for many appreciative audiences. When he plays, you can feel in every note he strikes the love and gratitude he has for his ability and for the music itself. His inspiration touches the hearts of all who hear him.

Your Purpose Is Beyond Your Goals

Inspiration, creative power, and energy flow into you when you attune yourself to the infinite.
— Paramahansa Yogananda

• Your purpose is your heart and soul's guiding direction for life.

• Anything you can accomplish isn't your purpose; accomplishments are stepping-stones.

• Your goals are the necessary stepping-stones to help you fulfill your true purpose.

• All accomplishment is transient, so strive unremittingly toward a lasting purpose.

Your purpose is beyond your goals. It's beyond your life. It's the vibrant vision and harmonizing voice resonating with your inner mind. Your purpose is a lifelong vision. Even if you act out only part of this vision during your lifetime, the whole world will be dazzled by your expression of genius.

The goals and objectives you achieve while fulfilling

your purpose build your stairway to the stars. The accomplishment of each goal is guaranteed to involve both benefits and drawbacks, and the more grateful you are for what you learn and receive, the more inspired you are to build your next step.

I remember consulting with three young entrepreneurs who owned and operated a computer software company. They scheduled a consultation because they felt that they'd already achieved their vision for their company and didn't know where to go from there. They were losing interest in the day-to-day operations, and their profits were lower than they had been in 12 years.

When I met with them, I realized that what they had been calling their vision was actually just a long-term goal they had set when they created their company. This goal was to become a million-dollar company. Now that they had reached that milestone, they thought they had reached the top of their company's ability.

We worked together to create an inspired vision-and-purpose statement, and when we had finished, they realized that becoming a million-dollar company was just the first big step toward becoming a global company. But beyond that next objective, they defined their purpose as being a software company that consistently identifies emerging needs in computing and meets those needs, whether or not they appear possible!

Once they had a vision that was bigger than they were, and a mission that could be worked on for life, they became inspired, motivated into action, and alive with creative ideas once again.

Dedicate Your Life to Your Purpose

*Commitment unlocks the doors of imagination, allows vision,
and gives us the right stuff to turn our dreams into reality.*
— James Womack

- When you dedicate, commit, or will your life to your purpose, the universe immediately begins to support and reward you.

- You're guided along your path when you listen consistently to your inner voice and focus on your inner vision.

- When you concentrate and focus on your purpose, you develop a clear picture of your success.

- When you're locked on to your purpose, every cell in your body joins to work as a winning team, assisting you in fulfilling your mission and rewarding you with health and vitality.

When you dedicate your life to an inspired purpose, everything becomes more meaningful, and you experience the fullness that life is intended to offer. On the other side of the coin, when you're not fulfilling your inspiration, living can feel like an aimless wandering in the desert of your senses, reacting to your circumstances and surroundings as if you were at their mercy. Questions like: *Is this all there is?* and *Why do I feel like something is missing from my life?* provide the perfect motivation and starting point for getting in touch with your life's calling. Once you discover your unique mission and commit to fulfilling it with definite action, you're on your way to the life you'd love to be living!

In physics, anything not fulfilling its intended purpose self-destructs. It's the universe's way of recycling energy. The same holds true for people. When we're not fulfilling our inspirations, we find ourselves living lives of desperation, creating turmoil in our minds and diseases in our bodies. These results aren't punishments, they're simply the effects of not using what we have or doing what we love to do. They're messages that let us know we're off course mentally.

About ten years ago, I consulted with a woman named Michelle. She had been working as a teacher's assistant in an adult literacy program, but her true desire was to be one of the teachers. "I love to read, and I know I can help other people learn how. I listen to what the other teachers say, and I know I can do it. Plus, I have some ideas of my own," she said, smiling.

I asked Michelle what stood in the way of her pursuing her calling to help other people learn to read, and she explained that she had become pregnant in high school and never received her diploma. She lost her vision to become a teacher, one thing led to another, and basically she believed that it was too late to pursue her inspired calling. To her, it was now a lost dream of the past.

"Michelle," I asked, "how many years do you intend to live?" She gave me a funny look, a little surprised by my question, and then she answered, "Well, I'm only 31. I hope to live at least another 50 years." "Okay," I said, "now how long would it take you to pass a high school equivalence test?"

"I could probably pass one by the end of the year," she replied.

"So that's one year. Plus about four more to earn a bachelor's degree in education." She nodded her head. "So let's see," I said, "that leaves 45 years to teach!"

I met with Michelle once more after that to help her create an action plan. Once she committed to her purpose and was inspired about her calling in life, she was unstoppable! Today she has her bachelor's degree in education and her teaching certificate.

The Truth Is . . .

Every calling is great, when greatly pursued.
— Oliver Wendell Holmes, Jr.

- When your highest priority is to follow the guidance of your heart and soul, you hear your inner wisdom.

- Your inspired purpose permeates all of your cells with love, and its grateful driving force causes courageous actions and services that create success and fulfillment.

- A definite purpose is one of the clearest and brightest roads to health.

- When you commit your life to your inspired calling, you leave an immortal effect on the world.

Reflections

The purpose of life is a life of purpose.
— Robert Byrne

This exercise will help you get in touch with your inspirations. Allow at least 20 minutes the first time you complete this Reflection. (You may choose to repeat this exercise. Each time you do, you'll remember more details and gain new insights.) Read all the instructions before beginning.

Sit in a comfortable chair with your feet flat on the floor and your arms in a relaxed position. Control your breathing by inhaling for five to ten seconds, then exhaling for five to ten seconds. (Select the period of time that feels most natural and comfortable to you.) Continue breathing in this one-to-one inhaling and exhaling ratio. Close your eyes.

While your eyes are closed, imagine yourself walking into a theater with a large screen at the front. You're the only person in the theater and may sit in any seat you desire.

Once you're seated, push the start button on the arm of your chair. Your life movie, beginning with the first day that you remember of this lifetime, will begin playing.

Sit back and enjoy the moments of your life. Pay particular attention to the moments that make you smile. Laugh and cry with joy. Feel inspired. Your movie will continue up to this day, this moment.

Now, before opening your eyes, thank yourself, thank the people in your life, and be thankful for all that you are, do, and have.

Realizations

To achieve great things,
we must live as though we are never going to die.
— Luc de Clapiers de Vauvenargues

Write your declaration, or statement, of purpose. Write what your heart calls you to do for life:

I, _____ *,*
hereby declare before myself and others that my primary
purpose in life is to be: _____

_____

_____

_____

by doing _____

_____

_____

_____

so I may have: _____

_____

_____

_____

Signed,

Read your purpose statement every day. Carry it with you, update it, and revise it until it becomes your life's masterpiece. Let this statement be your master plan for life. Listen wisely to your heart, and it will align you with what you know inwardly is your life's purpose.

Affirmations

- *I commit my life to my inspired purpose. I am leaving an immortal effect on the world.*

- *My heart and soul guide me to take wise action steps and inspire me with unconditional love.*

- *I am grateful for all that I am, all that I do, and all that I have.*

- *I am fulfilling my inspired purpose, and every cell of my body is healing and participating in my journey of unconditional love.*

Chapter 10

You're Never Given a Problem You Can't Solve

A problem is a chance for you to do your best.
— Duke Ellington

Where's the Silver Lining?

E very cloud has a silver lining and finding it is one of the most reliable ways to turn an apparent problem into a blessing! True wisdom is the ability to see the equal benefit or blessing hidden in every challenge, situation, sickness, or crisis. The silver lining is always as bright as the cloud is dark. And when we see its shining light, we're grateful for the gift of our challenge.

When life is flowing smoothly, we enjoy taking credit for its many opportunities. When we encounter what looks like a problem, we tend to look for reasons outside ourselves. But when we delve deeper, we discover that what seemed like a problem is actually an opportunity. The way for us to see the opportunity is to lift ourselves to a higher point of view. When we learn to accept—not deny—responsibility for the way we think and feel about daily experiences, we can open our minds to the guidance of our heart and soul.

We're never presented with a so-called problem unless we can solve it, either by ourselves or with the help of others. An orderly universe doesn't hand a child struggling with addition and subtraction a complex problem in calculus and demand that the child answer its riddle. We're only gifted with challenges for which we're prepared, so it's actually an honor to be handed a complex challenge. It's our chance to show that we're capable of finding the silver lining and experiencing more benefits and more love. When problems appear in our lives, we benefit from knowing that they're intended to serve a purpose. They're filled with rich information and many hints of what we'd love to be doing.

Three or four years ago, I received a phone call from one of my students. Carol said that she had just been fired from her position in retail management and was so caught up in her emotions that she was having a hard time seeing anything but her own despair.

I asked Carol if that position had been a fulfilling one for her. "No, not really," she said. "I've always known that some day I'd love to work on costumes for Broadway plays, but it takes a long time to break into that business. My retail job was a good one, and I was hoping to keep it until I was ready to move on."

I asked how her position had helped her move closer to her future goals, and she replied that her knowledge of clothing trends and styles had grown in her retail work. But she also said that she missed using her tailoring skills and was anxious to learn more about historical garments from 1900 and before. "Carol," I asked, "is this an opportunity for you to do that?"

For the first time in our conversation, her voice lifted: "Hey, maybe it is!" She began to list the types of positions that would give her more experience and knowledge about historical clothing. She also decided to center her search in New York so she could be closer to Broadway. What seemed like a problem and a disappointment just a few minutes before was turning into a great opportunity. Carol said that she'd devise her game plan and then would begin taking action steps within three days of our conversation.

Less than three months after she and I talked, she sent me a note to say that she'd just accepted a position in the division of historical textiles and clothing in a prominent museum just hours from Manhattan.

Every Problem Is an Opportunity to Learn and to Love

> *Problems are messages.*
> — Shakti Gawain

- Problems are designed to help you grow and evolve.

- You always have at least four choices—this, that, both, or neither.

- When you're grateful for what is, as it is, what appeared to be a problem is transformed into an event that you can love unconditionally.

As you travel through life and take on the challenges presented by difficult experiences, love dissolves your fears and gives you greater strength. Your experiences are tests on the path of evolution, and each lesson presents you with a new opportunity to learn and to experience unconditional love. But when your mind exaggerates the challenge, your thoughts are dominated or run by the situation rather than by you!

The reality is that problems are gifts. They give you a chance to walk from the darkness and heaviness of fear into the brightness and lightness of love. Once you learn that your heart and soul guide you toward whatever you need to resolve the situation, you'll know that there are really no problems, only opportunities to learn another lesson in love.

I recently received a thank-you letter from Susan, who, together with her husband, had consulted with me a few months earlier. The letter detailed her perception of how her marital problem had turned into a blessing. She wrote:

> I felt my whole world fall apart when I discovered one morning that my husband had an affair while I was pregnant with our fifth child. I'd been living an illusion that I was happily married to a professional, with a beautiful country home and five wonderful children. I'd made myself believe it was the fairy-tale existence that every little girl dreamed of. (Underneath, though, I knew that all had not been right with our relationship since the time our second child was born.)
>
> Still, when I found out about the affair, I was devastated. It was like everything I'd ever believed in was taken away. It was like every promise and vow had been broken, every truth I'd ever believed in was false, and my life had been nothing but a big lie.

But Susan went on to say that finding out about the affair had been exactly the jolt she needed to wake her from this self-made illusion.

> *Now, after completing The Demartini Method, that you shared with us, I'm truly thankful for the affair. I'm still married, and I now see the benefits in him, in myself, and in our relationship. I see that it was a lesson I had to learn, and there are no words of gratitude that can express my thankfulness to him for bringing my illusion to my awareness. Your Demartini Method, is a tool that helped me see a hidden perfection. It's a truly inspiring gift. Thank you Dr. John!*

Maximum Growth Occurs at the Border of Order and Chaos

> *For know that each Soul constantly meets its own self.*
> *No problem may be run away from. Meet it now.*
> — Edgar Cayce

- It's impossible to build without destroying, and equally impossible to destroy without building.

- You have the capacity to turn chaos into order and benefit from every problem.

- When you rise above your illusions of imbalance, you see a grand scheme and order.

- When you discover the benefits of your problem and study the lessons stored within it, your wisdom unfolds.

Problems can be wonderful transition points. Each trial is a potential stepping-stone to greatness. When we learn its lesson of love, we go on to the next lesson, which is generally more challenging as well as more rewarding. Just as passing each grade in school allows us to go up to a more challenging one, it also offers more rewarding benefits, and eventually graduation. Wise students of life welcome experiences that appear to offer adversity because every imaginary barrier is a personal challenge to grow, and with growth comes a greater sphere of influence, responsibility, and reward.

We discover who we are gradually, through experiences. With hindsight, what appeared to have been the greatest problems are recognized as occurring during the times of greatest growth and self-awareness. This principle holds true not only for individuals, but also for organizations, corporations, countries, the world, and beyond. When we find ourselves, individually or collectively, at the border between order and chaos, we're poised to experience the greatest growth and evolution.

Years ago, a man named Tom took part in The Breakthrough Experience. Tom's home and nearly all of his belongings had been destroyed in a San Francisco earthquake. He was very well insured and was going to be fine financially, but he had been shaken by the loss of so many items that held memories and meaning for him.

He said that in some ways, he felt like he was going through an identity crisis: "All of a sudden my life is so complicated, and so simple at the same time. It feels strange not to own anything. I've always had a lot of things, even as a kid, and it's a weird feeling to be left with only a few bags of clothes, a lamp, and a mailbox!" Tom was silent for a few seconds, then added, "On the other hand, it's sort of a relief not to own anything. The only thing I'm responsible for right now is me!"

During the two-day program, Tom was able to sort through many of his emotions. He continued to find benefits in the destruction of his house, and he began to restructure his life the way he really wanted it to be. He decided to buy a small condo on the beach in Southern California and a townhouse in Boston, near his children and grandchildren. He also decided to enroll in a yoga class and begin fitness walking.

At the end of the program, Tom thanked each participant for sharing so much with him. "I never thought I'd be saying this, but I'm honestly grateful for the earthquake," he said. "It shook the life back into me, and reminded me of what's really important. I'm 63 years old, and this is the perfect time to streamline my life and spend more time with my family and the people I love."

The Truth Is . . .

Each handicap is like a hurdle in a
steeplechase and when you ride up to it,
if you throw your heart over, the horse will go along, too.
— Lawrence Bixby

- The universe is a balance of experiences, all designed to help you evolve and to lead you to a state of gratefulness for what is, as it is, so you can learn to love it.

- You're never given a problem you can't solve and learn to love, either by yourself or with the help of others.

- When you rise above a problem and look at it from a broader point of view, the answers become easier to recognize.

- There really are no problems—only opportunities to learn another lesson in love.

Reflections

When I am working on a problem,
I never think about beauty . . .
but when I have finished,
if the solution is not beautiful,
I know it is wrong.
— R. Buckminster Fuller

1. Think of a situation that, when you first encountered it, appeared to be a big problem, but ultimately turned out to be a blessing in disguise.

2. Recall a time when you successfully solved a problem with the help of others.

3. Recall your last traumatic experience.

4. Think of at least three ways you've grown as a result of that event.

Realizations

It is not always by plugging away at a difficulty and sticking to it that one overcomes it, often it is by working on the one next to it. Some things and some people have to be approached obliquely, at an angle.
— André Gide

1. Summarize a situation you experienced in the past, which seemed to be a big problem or drama at the time.

2. List five ways that the problem you described has benefited you and helped you grow.

3. Summarize a situation you are currently experiencing, which appears to be a problem.

4. List five ways you can benefit from this so called problem.

Affirmations

*   *When I'm faced with what looks like a problem, I open my heart to the silence within.*

*   *When I accept responsibility for my daily experiences, I open my heart and mind to guidance from my inner voice.*

*   *I am a being of magnificence and beauty.*

- *My health problems are challenges to love; I have everything I need to heal.*

Chapter 11

Inspiration Is the Secret of Vitality

*And the Lord God formed man of the dust of the ground,
and breathed into his nostrils the breath of life;
and man became a living Soul.*
— Genesis 2:7

Are You Full of Life . . . or "Barely Breathing"?

Inspiration is the breath of life. It's necessary for physical, mental, and spiritual health and vitality. From the first inspiring breath at birth, your body relies on breathing to function. From your first conscious thought, your mind relies on inspiration from your heart and soul to be motivated into action.

Your life's vitality is a reflection of your level of inspiration, just as your physical breathing is a reflection of your mental condition. Long exhalations and short inhalations tell you that you're emotionally depressed. When you have long inhalations and short exhalations, you're elated. When the ratio of inhalations to exhalations is balanced, you're centered, poised, and in a state of grateful, unconditional love.

I once received a call from Kathy, a student of mine, who was experiencing an emotional depression but wasn't sure what was causing it. I asked her if she could pinpoint when she began feeling depressed, and she said that it had begun about two weeks before she called me. I asked her what was happening in her life, and Kathy said that her job was fine, her kids were great, and she and her husband, who are both high school teachers, were really enjoying their summer vacation.

She said, "Other than not being able to run, everything is fine." Kathy explained that she had injured her ankle a few weeks earlier and hadn't been able to run the five or six miles she was accustomed to each day. She knew that part of her depression was caused by the lack of exercise, but she didn't realize that this lack of balanced aerobic breathing was a primary cause as well.

I explained to Kathy that when she runs five or six miles, she's probably maintaining a balanced breath for more than 45 minutes a day. I suggested that until she was able to run again, she might take 15 minutes, twice a day, to practice balanced, rhythmic breathing while sitting or lying down. I also recommended that she read inspiring books and articles, look for the benefits she was deriving from her temporary ankle injury, and appreciate them.

Less than two weeks later, Kathy called back to say that the balanced-breathing sessions were working well: "I feel energized again, and what's really great is that my ankle seems to be healing faster! Thanks, Dr. Demartini!"

Gratitude Opens Your Heart to Inspiration

*If you haven't got all the things you want,
be grateful for the things you don't have that you don't want.*
— Anonymous

- When you thank yourself and others, you open your heart to your inspiration.

- Taking time each day for balanced breathing and meditation puts you in tune with your inspired vibration and energy.

- Energy and vitality are infinite when you recognize and appreciate their source: a heart filled with gratitude.

- Inspiring messages are available at every moment; just be truly grateful and listen with your heart.

When you're grateful, you're centered, and you literally "breathe easily." At these moments, your heart is open and you're receptive or tuned in to the messages of your heart and soul. That's why gratitude is such an important part of our lives. It's the doorway to inspiration and unconditional love!

When I was a little boy, my mother and father used to say, "Count your blessings, son." At that time, I didn't realize how much wisdom they were revealing to me. I knew that they were telling me that I should appreciate what I had, but I didn't know why. And I definitely didn't know that what I was thankful for would grow. But as I got older and began to see and experience the power of being grateful, I began to understand the depth of the profound guidance my parents had lovingly offered to me as a child. What a gift of life they gave me!

Today, when I wake up in the morning and before I go to sleep at night, I count my blessings, and I listen for the wisdom of my heart and soul.

As Your Breath Wanders, So Does Your Mind

Wisdom is not wisdom when it is derived from books alone.
— Horace

- When your breathing is relaxed and rhythmic, your mind is calm and clear.

- Balanced breathing generates power and vitality, and poises your body for healing.

- Controlling your breathing quiets the brain noise and creates inner peace and serenity.

- The oxygen you inhale provides energy to your cells for optimum performance and healing.

Mastering your breath is the secret to mastering your mind and increasing your inspiration and vitality. Deep, rhythmic breathing is your lungs' inspiring gift for health and well-being. While it isn't possible, or necessary, to expand your lungs totally with every breath, a really complete breath is an inspiration. Complete rhythmic breathing should be practiced periodically to fill your lungs to capacity and to take in great amounts of life force from the air. When you first practice breathing like this, you'll begin to feel the benefits almost immediately.

I remember a man in one of my yoga classes being a little startled by the sensation of warm, flowing energy he experienced when he first practiced complete and balanced breathing. Chuck was an advertising executive whose wife enrolled him in the class because she was worried about his stress level and wanted him to learn to relax. He admitted that he felt like a bundle of nerves: "The more uptight I get, the harder it is for me to focus on my job and think of creative ideas. And when that happens, I *really* get tense, and then I can't think of anything!"

Chuck became a believer in balanced breathing after his first session, but he admits that he was skeptical at first. "If you'd told me that learning how to breathe a certain way could change my life, I would have laughed my way right out of your class!" he said. "But here I am one year later, and I'm the top account executive in my firm. I won two awards this year for creative advertising, and I feel younger and more relaxed than I've felt in years."

The Truth Is . . .

*Inspiration is everywhere. If you're ready to appreciate it,
an ant can be one of the wonders of the universe.*
— Anonymous

- Powerful people have powerful breaths and are filled with creative energy.

- As your mind wanders, so does your breath; as your breath wanders, so does your mind.

- When you've mastered your breath, you've mastered your mind.

- When you've mastered your mind, you've liberated the source of your healing and vitality.

Reflections

Breathe on me, breath of God,
Fill me with a life anew,
That I may love what thou dost love,
And do what thou wouldst do.
— Edwin Hatch

This simple exercise creates harmony and balance throughout your central nervous system. To practice deep and rhythmic breathing, follow these five steps, which you can do while standing, sitting, or lying down:

1. Exhale deeply through your nose, contracting your stomach completely.

2. Inhale slowly through your nose, expanding your abdomen, then your chest, and then raising your shoulders up toward your ears.

3. Hold for a few comfortable seconds.

4. Exhale in the reverse pattern, slowly dropping your shoulders, relaxing your chest, and contracting your abdomen.

5. Repeat this pattern slowly, then fast, then faster still, until your face flushes; then slowly again, until your neck loosens and your mind steadies.

Realizations

The heart has its reasons, which reason knows nothing of.
— Blaise Pascal

Count your blessings. Look for people, things, or events that you can be grateful for, and silently continue to be thankful for them until you have inspired tears of unconditional love for the magnificence of the universe. Keep probing deeper into the beautiful order lying within the essence of your own life. Keep thanking until your tears of inspiration clean off the windows of your heart and soul and reveal their messages and visions. Then ask for a message of inspiration and write down whatever comes to you.

Affirmations

- *I am balancing and centering my breathing and balancing and centering my mind.*

- *Through my inspiration, energy is infinite and universally available.*

- *I am grateful for my many blessings.*

- *I am opening my heart to inspiration and healing.*

Chapter 12

A Healthy Mind Maintains a Healthy Body

Health is not a condition of matter; but of mind.
— Mary Baker Eddy

Are You Making Yourself Sick?

It's interesting that so many people know they can make themselves sick, but few people acknowledge that they can make themselves well. In my day-to-day interactions, I often hear statements like: "I was worried sick," or "I was so upset that I couldn't eat for days," or "It really broke my heart."

Our thoughts, perceptions, feelings, and words can make us sick. But they can also make us strong and help heal our bodies. When we have lopsided perceptions and see a situation or a person in our life as "all bad," our negative thoughts weaken our body's ability to function efficiently. But when we take our lopsided perceptions and bring them into perfect equilibrium by balancing the negatives with an equal amount of positives, we annihilate their power to create sickness and disease and we open our hearts to the unconditional love that heals.

Several years ago, a doctor named Chuck attended The Breakthrough Experience. At the time, he was recovering from radiation treatments that had been used to eliminate his laryngeal cancer. He left the program feeling energized and was once again inspired about his chiropractic practice.

About two years after Chuck attended the Breakthrough program, he called to tell me that the laryngeal cancer had returned. Worried and frightened, he called to schedule a one-on-one consultation.

When Chuck arrived, I asked him to tell me exactly where his physician had spotted the cancer. He said it was on his left vocal cord. I shared with Chuck that a cancerous growth on his vocal cord probably meant that he wasn't saying what he really felt. Because it was on the left cord, and since the left side of the body is the feminine side, I said that no doubt he had some blocks and lies associated with the women in his life.

For the next several hours, I worked with Chuck to help him shift his perceptions and see the balance in his feelings toward his mother, his stepdaughter, his sister, and his wife. I knew that when he saw the perfection in his feelings and experiences with the females in his life, he'd be able to say the things he couldn't say, and his body would be in the necessary balanced state to heal itself. By the end of our session, Chuck said he felt as if several heavy weights had been lifted, and he had such an overwhelming desire to say "Thank you" and "I love you" to his family members that he called them as soon as he returned home.

Two months later, when Chuck went back to his doctor

for the operation, the doctor saw that the cancer was gone. "I finally learned what it means to be truly grateful," Chuck said. "I still have both vocal cords, and I have so much in my life to be grateful for each and every day." It has been a year since then, and I recently received a letter from Chuck saying that he's healthy and doing what he loves to do.

Your Body Believes Every Word You Think and Say

The healing system is the way the body
mobilizes all its resources to combat disease.
The belief system is often the activator of the healing system.
— Norman Cousins

- Everything you think and say makes an impression on your mind and your body.

- When you think or say the same phrase over and over again, your mind and your body begin to believe it, whether you mean it or not.

- The emotional charges of fear and guilt are stored in your muscles and organs and affect your health as long as you believe in their illusions.

- It's almost useless to treat functional disorders until your mind has found inner balance and peace through unconditional love.

One of the most immediate ways to change your health is to change your thoughts and words. Listen to what you're thinking and saying. If you say them often enough, your mind and body will begin to believe statements like: "This job is killing me," or "I can't stand her," and "He makes me sick."

Frequently we make statements out of anger or frustration, which we end up believing instead of opening our hearts to the truth and wisdom of love. The longer we continue to believe our own lies, the more impact those lies have on our life and health and the more deeply they affect us.

That was the case with a married couple I worked with about 12 years ago. They came to my office because their 49-year-old daughter, Susan, begged them to talk with me.

Susan was a client of mine, and she believed that I could help her parents. Robert and Mary had been married for nearly 50 years, and Susan told me that they had been arguing her entire life. They were both in the final stages of cancer, and Susan wanted them to reconcile with each other before they died.

Before the three of us were even seated in my office, Mary and Robert were arguing. They traded insults back and forth and blamed each other for a variety of things that occurred earlier in the day. Then Mary turned to me and said, "I don't know why we're here. You can't help us. We've been fighting like cats and dogs for 50 years because he's stubborn, selfish, and intolerable!"

Robert crossed his arms and said, "Well I may be stubborn and selfish, but you're the one who's intolerable. You've been a miserable bitch of a wife, and nobody can make you happy!"

This exchange continued until I suggested that we look back to the time when the two of them decided to get married. "Did you love each other then?" I asked. They agreed that they did, or they wouldn't have gotten married.

"So what was it that created such anger between the two of you?" I asked.

They looked at each other, then back at me. Finally, Mary said, "We were only married three months when he got me pregnant, and I had to quit my job and stay home with the baby! I didn't want to have a baby until we were married at least two or three years. He ruined everything, and I've been mad at him ever since!"

Robert said, "I tried to help her with Susan, but I was working two jobs to make ends meet, and after a while I didn't even want to go home at night. Every day she complained about something else."

"So, let me get this straight," I said. "The two of you have been mad at each other for 50 years because Susan was born two years sooner than you wanted her?" Mary nodded, and Robert shrugged. I knew that the love was still there. It was just covered up with so many years of denial and conflict that they couldn't feel it anymore.

I asked them to hold hands, look into each other's eyes, and say "Thank you" and "I love you" to each other. At first they refused, but with a good bit of encouragement and after a few more rounds of verbal attacks, they held hands and looked into each other's eyes. When they did, their hearts began to soften, and they both began to cry. Robert finally hugged Mary and said, "I love you," and Mary said, "I love you, too," and they cried for several minutes.

Robert and Mary realized that all their anger, frustration, and bitterness grew over the years and eventually began to consume them both in the form of cancer. By the time they visited my office, Robert was partially dependent on a respirator, and Mary was too weak to continue with radiation therapy. But when they opened their hearts to each other and felt the love that had been there all along, they were thankful for the opportunity to live the remainder of their lives together in harmony.

Program Yourself for Health

*Once you have been confronted with a
life-and-death situation, trivia no longer matters.
Your perspective grows and you live at a deeper level.
There is no time for pettiness.*
— Margaretta Rockefeller

- Have certainty that the principles of healing will work for you.

- Healing comes from within, and everyone can heal themselves with unconditional love.

- The two greatest healers are laughter and tears, because they're the two sides of love.

- What the loving mind can conceive and believe, it can achieve.

Program yourself for health by thinking healthy thoughts, focusing on your improvements, and believing that soon you'll be in the state of health you desire. Watch funny movies; read inspirational stories and books; and fill your mind with powerful thoughts of strength, health, and vitality.

When I think of stories to illustrate this point, I often recall Edith, a woman in her 50s whose arthritis was so severe that she frequently had trouble walking. But one day I saw Edith walking in the park with a gentleman. At first, I almost didn't recognize her. She was walking so smoothly and smiling so brightly that she looked much younger.

When I ran into Edith again several weeks later, she told me that man I had seen her with was her new boyfriend. I mentioned how good her health appeared to be, and she agreed that she was enjoying a very pleasant and pain-free spring. I didn't see Edith again until late that summer, but when I did, her arthritis seemed to be worse than ever. She told me that her love affair had ended, and she was depressed and felt awful.

I asked Edith if she realized that her arthritic condition improved when her state of mind improved. She agreed that her body had felt much better when she felt content with her life. But she said that she wasn't interested in trying anymore.

"Edith," I said, "you're the one who made yourself better the last time; you can do it again. Picture yourself walking through the park with a new boyfriend, or playing with one of your grandchildren."

She smiled when I mentioned her grandchildren and agreed that she would try. I didn't see Edith for months after that, but one day I received a package, in which Edith had sent a beautiful seashell with a note:

> Greetings! I picked this up myself this morning when my grandson Brandon and I took a walk on the beach. Thank you, Dr. Demartini. You were right! I have the power to improve my health.

The Truth Is . . .

Reality is something we rise above.
— Liza Minnelli

- Unconditional love heals.

- When you're grateful and loving, your body is healthy and strong.

- You have the power to create both sickness and health in your mind and body.

- Your body speaks to you with illness to give you another opportunity to love yourself and others.

- When you're humble and grateful, your heart is open, and the healing power of unconditional love flows through you.

Reflections

Humor is a rich and versatile source of power—
a spiritual resource very like prayer.
— Marilyn R. Chandler

1. Recall the last time you made yourself sick with anger, frustration, anxiety, fear, or guilt.

2. Make a commitment to listen to your thoughts and words. Weed out phrases like: "It makes me

sick . . ." "I can't stand it . . . " "My feet are killing me . . . " "That drives me crazy . . ." and so on.

3. Clear your mind. Take 15 minutes each day to sit with your eyes closed and practice relaxed breathing. Slowly breathe in through your nose to a count of six or seven, then exhale slowly to the same count. The idea is to balance your inhaling and exhaling in a one-to-one ratio. Some people will feel most comfortable inhaling only four or five seconds, and others will feel comfortable inhaling much longer. Find the rate that makes you feel most relaxed and comfortable.

4. At least once each day, think about all the things for which you are grateful, until you feel tears of gratitude come to your eyes. Then visualize and feel the warm and soothing sensation of unconditional love filling your body with healing energy.

Realizations

Many things cause pain, which would cause pleasure if you regarded their advantages.
— Baltasar Gracián y Morales

1. List any conditions you'd love to heal.

2. Number the conditions on your list according to their urgency or priority; number one should be the condition with the highest priority.

3. Write 30 ways the condition you chose as number one is serving you.

4. Write an openhearted letter of thanks for the blessings of your sickness and your health.

Affirmations

- *I am grateful, my heart is open, and the healing power of unconditional love is filling my body.*

- *I am nourishing my mind with healthy thoughts.*

- *I love and respect my body as my most dedicated and loyal friend.*

- *Both my health and my sickness are blessings and opportunities for me to love myself and others.*

- *Whatever I can conceive and believe, my mind can achieve.*

Chapter 13

Overindulge in Moderation

You have all the willpower in the world to break any habit.
The power of divine will is always with you,
and can never be destroyed.
— Paramahansa Yogananda

Do You Have Passions . . . or Do They Have You?

The opportunity to enjoy life's pleasures is a blessing, and we're wise to be grateful for our gifts. But if we follow only our passions and let them run our lives, we may easily be sidetracked from pursuing our inspirations. Tangents, sickness, and infatuations can take us off course. Learning moderation is one of the most effective ways to free yourself from addictions and turn unhealthy habits into healthy ones.

When you indulge your passions with moderation, they're satisfied, and you're in control. When you allow yourself to overindulge in them, they're in control, and your extremes lead to other mental and physical imbalances.

127

It's not unusual to swing back and forth between opposite behaviors at times, but when you moderate your swings and seek the balanced center, you experience a healthier, more productive life.

Chances are that you have a habit or two you'd like to eliminate. But often when you try to eliminate something, you end up exaggerating it instead. A great example of this concept is a man named Joe who used to be an alcoholic. Joe first met with me five or six years ago when he realized that alcohol was running his life. He had tried counseling, as well as Alcoholics Anonymous, but he said that the thought of never taking another drink generally led him to a bar or a liquor store. "The last time I said I'd never take another drink, it lasted for one day, and then I drove to the liquor store, bought a pint of scotch, and drank the whole thing," Joe said. "I don't know what to do, and I know I have to do something!"

First, I helped Joe balance his lopsided perception of alcohol and his attachment to drinking. He listed all the ways that drinking benefited him. Then he listed an equal number of ways that drinking was a drawback. He quickly began to see that drinking was neither right nor wrong; it was simply drinking.

Once Joe understood this concept he said, "One of the reasons I end up getting drunk is because I feel so guilty about not being able to stop drinking. I was going around in circles with this!" He'd been caught in a vicious cycle, and his feelings of guilt about his drinking and his fear that he couldn't stop were literally ruining his life.

I explained to Joe that the wisest way to gain control of a habit or addiction was to moderate it. "But," he said, "I thought that once you were an alcoholic, you were always an alcoholic. If I quit for a while, won't I want to go right back to drinking every day again, once I take that first drink?" Joe and I spent the remainder of the session exploring that question, and he realized that he'd never really tried moderation in the way I was suggesting. He decided that he was comfortable with the idea of drinking every other day. His long-term goal was to drink only on occasion, but he wanted to begin with a step he felt certain that he could achieve. Joe and I devised an action plan to support him in keeping his commitment to himself.

When Joe walked into my office a month later, he seemed like a different person. He carried himself with pride and he looked several inches taller! He proudly told me that for the first two weeks he kept his commitment to drinking only every other day, except one weekend when he drank both Friday and Saturday nights. "But," he said, "it was okay, because instead of feeling guilty about it, I just decided that Sunday would be a no-alcohol day, and I'd be right on schedule again!"

I congratulated Joe on his first two weeks and asked him about the other two weeks. "Well," he said, "when I saw that I could drink only four days out of seven, I knew that I could cut that back to drinking only three days out of seven, so that's what I've been doing!"

Joe said that his plan for the following month was to reduce the number of drinking days to two a week, as well as to moderate the amount of alcohol he drank on those days.

Joe proved to himself that he could succeed and keep his own promises. His self-worth increased, and his self-discipline climbed right along with it! Joe has now been an "occasional drinker" for more than four years, and he credits moderation for his success.

Moderation Is the Secret to a Healthy Mind and Body

Never eat more than you can lift.
— Miss Piggy

- Moderation creates mental and physical balance.

- When you make overindulgence a habit, your mind and body communicate their distress with sickness, depression, and anxiety.

- Passions are not to be condemned, just moderated.

- Moderation is one of life's most potent healers.

Variety may give life its spice, but it's moderation that provides us with healthy equilibrium and rhythm. Our bodies and minds are designed to work most efficiently when we're living a balanced life of moderation. When we choose to overwork, overplay, overeat, overdrink, overexert, or overdo anything else, we throw ourselves off balance, and sooner or later our minds and bodies pay the price.

I met a woman named Deborah at an educational conference a few years ago. She had accomplished a great deal in her career in a short period of time, but she confided that she didn't know how long she could maintain the pace she'd been keeping. Her average work week was 70 hours or more, and she spent very little time taking care of herself and her own needs. Consequently, her lifestyle was starting to take its toll. As we talked, she mentioned that during the past year she had been sick frequently, had gained 15 pounds, and was suffering from allergies that she'd never had before. Deborah was running herself into the ground. She understood that she'd be healthier mentally and physically if she moderated her work hours and devoted some time to the other areas of her life. But she was afraid that if she slowed down, she'd lose her current footing and status in her school district.

I helped Deborah understand that the people who are the most fulfilled and successful all around are those who live balanced lives of moderation. I explained that if she took the time for exercise, proper nutrition, and adequate rest, her productivity would increase rather than decrease.

Last year I received a note from Deborah telling me that she was exercising again, had taken off the extra pounds, felt better, and had just received a promotion.

Nothing of the Senses Can Satisfy the Soul

> *Man's many desires are like the small*
> *metal coins he carries about in his pocket.*
> *The more he has, the more they weigh him down.*
> — Satya Sai Baba

- If physical life was your sole purpose, a mere existence would be satisfying.

- Anything that's perceived as good and pleasurable, which stimulates opiate release and gives a "high," can become addictive.

- Excesses stunt personal and spiritual growth.

- Moderation and balance enhance personal and spiritual growth.

Henry James wisely said, "The infinite hunger of a soul cannot be satisfied with the things of sense." In other words, no matter how much or how often we eat, drink, shop, have sex, or anything else that pleases us physically, it won't satisfy our heart and soul's inspirations. There's nothing bad or wrong with pleasing ourselves physically, especially when we do it in moderation. But our heart and soul's hunger is fed when we live a grateful and inspired life devoted to our ultimate mission or purpose.

People are often driven to excesses by an internal feeling that something's missing from their lives. But that something can't be found in material possessions or earthly delights, even if these things seem to fill the void temporarily. The feeling of a void is created when you tune out the love and guidance from your heart and soul. But when you tap in to the guidance and unconditional love of your inner knowing, you're fulfilled at a deeper level, and your physical excesses can be more easily moderated.

One of my favorite examples to illustrate this point is a surfer I met when I was 17 and living on the north shore of Oahu. The other surfers affectionately referred to him as Death Wish, but his real name was Dan. He got his nickname because he had a large collection of self-destructive habits that he indulged in to excess. Every day he drank at least a six-pack of beer and smoked a pack or two of cigarettes; he shunned healthy food, rarely drank water, and would take just about any risk suggested to him. One night while heading into town for dinner, I ran into Dan and asked him if he wanted to join me. We ended up in a pizza place, and for some reason, he decided to pour his heart out to me. He told me that no matter what he did or how much he did it, he couldn't get rid of the emptiness he felt inside. At that time, I didn't know what to say to Dan, but now I understand that the emptiness he was feeling was the result of his having tuned out his inner voice in an attempt to fill the void with acts of desperation instead of acts of inspiration.

The Truth Is . . .

A man who has not passed through the inferno
of his passions has never overcome them.
— Carl Jung

- Moderation is wisdom.

- A moderate, balanced lifestyle creates a productive, healthy life.

- When you obey your heart's and soul's guidance and follow your inspirations, you experience fulfillment.

- When you ignore your heart's and soul's guidance and follow the extremes of your passions, you experience emptiness.

Reflections

Moderation is a tree with roots of contentment
and fruits of tranquility and peace.
— North African saying

1. Recall the most recent occasion when you allowed yourself to overdo it in some way.

2. Recall the thoughts you had about yourself and the occasion—both during and afterward.

3. What did your thoughts lead you to feel or do?

4. Think of three benefits and three drawbacks of your experience.

Realizations

Self-respect is the fruit of discipline;
the sense of dignity grows with the ability to say no to oneself.
— Abraham J. Heschel

1. List three of the activities or extreme passions in which you overindulge.

2. Select the extreme passion you feel has the greatest influence on you, then write ten ways that your overindulgence or extreme passion benefits you and ten ways that it's a drawback.

3. Decide on your ultimate goal in moderating your behavior and write it down. Example: *I overindulge in chocolate.* Then you might write: *When it comes to my passion for chocolate, I'd love to eat one or two wonderful pieces of chocolate each week.*

4. Determine the first step to take in order to moderate your behavior and make a firm and loving commitment to yourself to keep your word. Make sure it's a step that you're certain you can achieve.

Affirmations

*   *I am feeding my heart and soul with my inspirations and by doing what I love to do.*

*   *I am moderating my extreme passions and living a healthier life.*

*   *I am a master of moderation, and my life is balanced and centered.*

*   *I am grateful for the lessons that my passions have taught me because they demonstrate the power of moderation.*

Chapter 14

Money Withers When It's Hoarded

Can anybody remember when the times
were not hard, and money not scarce?
— Ralph Waldo Emerson

Is Your Money Lying Around While You're Hard at Work?

People who think of money as a finite resource have a tendency to hoard it rather than invest it, save it with interest, and use it wisely to pursue their inspired dreams. People who have faith in themselves, however, appreciate what they have and are certain that they can earn more. These people demonstrate confidence and don't block their attraction of wealth with fear, doubt, sickness, or insecurity.

The more you value something, the more you dread its loss. Sometimes people block wealth and prosperity because they put an exaggerated value on it. It's important to remember that both wealth and poverty offer their own unique pains and pleasures. One isn't necessarily any easier than the other, but realistically it's much more challenging to reach your highest dreams when you block the attraction of financial resources.

One day I met a man named Joe in Central Park in New York. Joe was selling ice cream, and we started talking. He asked what I did, and I told him that I was a professional speaker.

He looked off into the distance and said, "You know, I'm more than the ice cream man!" I told Joe that I believed everyone was more than the job they were doing and asked if there was something else he'd love to be doing instead.

"Are you kidding?" he asked. "Who the hell wouldn't love to be doing anything but this? My dream is to buy some land, start an organic herb farm, and get very rich!"

I told him that I thought that sounded like a good plan, and I asked him what he was doing to pursue it. Joe explained that he couldn't do anything to pursue it without money. I offered some suggestions about saving and investing money so that he could achieve his dream one day. He seemed interested at first but then said: "It all sounds great, but you know as well as I do that some people have the money, and the other people want the money. I'm one of the guys who wants the money. Unless I hit the lottery, I'll be the ice cream man until I retire or find something else to do! But don't worry about Joe. I've got a nice little nest egg I keep in the safety of my apartment, and nobody can take that away from me. But thanks for the walk down fantasy lane, mister."

Joe was convinced that he was incapable of generating the money he needed to pursue his dream, and he was content to stash money in his apartment, without earning any interest, because he didn't have enough faith in himself or in banks to invest it. He had simply given up on his dream, when the reality is that he could accomplish his vision if he just believed in himself and put his energy, resources, mind, and heart into it.

To Make Your Assets Grow, Keep Them in Motion

Do not value money for any more or any less than it's worth;
it is a good servant, but a bad master.
— Alexandre Dumas

- Money must circulate to grow.

- You must spend money and save money to make money.

- It makes no difference how much you make; the secret lies in how well you manage what you have.

- The law of fair exchange means you won't get something for nothing.

Money is a form of energy, and energy in motion is more productive than energy at rest. When you save money and spend it wisely, you make your money grow. Whether you make $15,000 or $1 million a year, you need to learn to manage what you have efficiently, and to be grateful for it, before you'll receive more. That's one of the most basic laws of accumulating wealth. The other fundamental law is the Golden Rule of cause and effect, or fair exchange. The old adages "What you sow, you reap" and "You get what you pay for" are filled with wisdom.

When I was in professional school, I knew a man named Sal who owned a little corner store a few miles away. Sometimes I took a break from my research and studies to walk to his store to clear my mind and pick up a few things that I needed. It seemed as though Sal was there no matter when I stopped in, at any time of the day or night.

"Don't you ever go home?" I once teased him.

Sal didn't see the humor in my question. "I'd love to go home," he said, raising his voice. "But I've got bills up to my ears, and no matter how hard I work, I barely stay ahead."

Sal went on to talk about his monthly expenses and high-interest debts. He also mentioned that he never seemed to have enough money from his business to contribute to his own retirement fund. "I'm 54, and I'm gonna have to keep at it until I drop dead, I guess," he said.

For some reason, even after several weeks had passed, I continued to think about Sal. One day while walking to class, I noticed a bright yellow flyer on a bulletin board that advertised a financial-management class. I felt that somehow my conversation with Sal had sparked a new awareness of my own need to learn to manage my money.

The woman offering the all-day seminar had made most of her money with investments, and she was very knowledgeable about some of the basic principles of money management that had stood the test of time and led to her own prosperity. I enrolled in the class, and what I learned in eight hours was worth at least three times the cost of the course.

The most profound principle I learned that day was

that one of the most successful paths to wealth is the path of an inspired dream. When we have a mission or a purpose bigger than we are, and our vision stretches beyond our own lifetime, we become like magnets attracting the resources we require to fulfill our inspirations.

I still thank Sal for starting me on my quest for financial freedom. He gave me a great gift. He helped me see a potential circumstance in my own business someday. Seeing that picture motivated me into action. Thanks to Sal, and many others, I've become adept in financial management.

There's an old bit of wisdom that says: "If you want the light, you must pass the torch." Today, I'm passing the torch by teaching my own Secrets of Financial Mastery program so that others may be blessed with the information and knowledge of money management that has been of such benefit for me and my mission.

When You Invest Wisely in Yourself and Others, Your Riches Multiply

Never invest your money in anything that eats or needs repairing
— Billy Rose

- Pay yourself first.

- Save at least 10 percent of what you earn.

- Invest in inspiration, not desperation.

- Don't pay the price of procrastination.

The wealthy pay themselves first. If you feel guilty about paying yourself first or receiving money for your services, you'd be wise to ask yourself why. The universe rewards those who reward others and themselves. When you spend and invest money wisely, it will return to you tenfold.

While many excellent investments exist, you're always wisest to invest in your inspirations. When you receive an inspired idea for yourself or your business, reward yourself by making a deposit in your savings account or putting more money toward an investment. When you invest in others' inspirations, do so anonymously. That way, they'll send the thought of gratitude out into the world. You're rewarded in life by how many others you can help to be thankful.

Don't pay the price of procrastination. Time is money. Every day that you don't save is a day that you add more to your work. The price of procrastination is more than what it appears to be on the surface. For example, at a 10 percent annual rate of return, to have $1 million in your savings account when you reach age 65, you only need to save about $100 a month—if you begin saving when you're 20 years old. If you begin saving at 30, you'll need to save about $200 a month. Waiting until you're 40, however, will require saving about $750 monthly to reach your goal of saving $1 million by age 65.

You can attract financial wealth and have a wonderful appreciation for your prosperity without allowing it to interfere with your personal and inspirational growth. When you keep your perception of money in balance and use it as a vehicle to pursue your inspirations and ultimate purpose, you allow wealth to flow into your life.

The Truth Is . . .

Money can't buy happiness, but neither can poverty.
— Anonymous

- The financial form of life's wealth is meant to be appreciated as a gift and used wisely.

- For it to stand, a kingdom of wealth must be built on a foundation of character and integrity.

- Your finances prosper when you begin to do what you're inspired—and most perfectly designed—to do.

- When you invest in your own and others' inspirations gratefully, you multiply your wealth.

Reflections

*I have enough money to last me the rest of my life,
unless I buy something.*
— Jackie Mason

1. Take a few moments to review your financial situation mentally.

2. Think of a circumstance in which you didn't pursue an inspired idea because you didn't believe that you could earn the money or attract the investors you needed.

3. Think of a situation when you were inspired about doing something for which you knew you didn't have the money, but you trusted yourself to create the money, and you succeeded.

4. Investigate your feelings and opinions about wealth. Question why you believe what you do and when you began to believe it.

Realizations

I find all this money a considerable burden.
— J. Paul Getty

Make three columns on a sheet of paper; write ten benefits of becoming wealthy, ten obstacles to becoming wealthy, and ten ways to surmount those obstacles.

Affirmations

- *I invest in my inspirations and give thanks for my investments.*

- *I appreciate the wealth I have and know that I can earn more.*

- *I am a master of finance, and money flows easily into my life.*

- *I am attracting the money and resources I desire to help my healing.*

Chapter 15

Inspired Service
Attracts Abundance
and Recognition

God loveth a cheerful giver.
— II Corinthians 9:7

Do You Give as Much as You Love to Receive?

To attract abundance and recognition, we must give inspired service. The more wisely we give, the more we receive. This universal principle is of paramount importance in our daily lives. When we're not receiving all the blessings we desire, it's because we're not sharing with others the blessings we have in a wise and openhearted way. When we want our income to grow, we must put our hearts and souls into our work. When we want our bodies to heal, we must put inspired energy into our desires and humble ourselves to give service to others. Only then will we receive richer rewards.

If we expect our dreams of abundance and recognition to materialize without the willingness to serve others, we're sure to be disappointed. We're like energy transformers and can accept only as much energy as we release. Put simply, we get what we'd love to have in life by helping others get what they'd love to have.

Frequently, people who don't possess the level of abundance or receive the amount of praise and recognition they'd like become disgruntled and bitter. A few years ago, I attended the retirement dinner of a CEO who had consulted with me several times concerning the leadership of his company. The last time Jim met with me, a few days prior to his retirement, he said, "I can't wait to get out of that place. I never made what I deserved, and I never got the recognition I deserved either!"

I suggested that Jim would be wise to balance his lopsided perceptions by using The Demartini Method. I knew that if he could see how his experience had served him, he could retire with gratitude rather than resentment.

At first he didn't believe that his experiences had served him at all, but over the next two hours, he began to see many benefits. He also began to recognize the part he'd played in creating the way that people treated him. When he left my office, he said, "Thanks, Dr. Demartini. I learned more today than I have in the last ten years. Thank God I met with you before my retirement dinner. I have an entirely different speech to give now."

There were about 50 people at the dinner, and from the conversation at the table at which I sat, I gathered that many people in the company were glad to see him go. He had a reputation for taking credit for others' accomplishments and for quickly placing blame on his subordinates. But when he stood up to give his speech, he projected so much grateful and loving energy that someone behind me whispered, "What's gotten into him?"

Jim cleared his voice and said, "Thank you. Thank you

for all the times when you covered for me when I was doing less than my best." Then he gave a few specific examples of times when he had passed on blame to others out of his own fear of reprimand from the board. He also thanked several people whom he said he hadn't acknowledged for work well done. Jim continued recognizing and thanking all the people who had helped him succeed, and when his voice cracked with emotion, there were tears all around the room.

When Jim humbled himself and gave thanks and appreciation to others, they in turn gave thanks and recognition to him. The same people who, only an hour earlier, were looking forward to his retirement more than he was, began thanking him. They thanked him for the times he had supported them and acknowledged him for the things he had done well.

You Rise in Glory as You Sink in Pride

Tell me what you brag about, and I'll tell you what you lack.
— Spanish proverb

- Humility keeps you from rising too high with elation and sinking too low with depression.

- Take no credit; take no blame. Just love.

- When you practice love and gratitude with humility, you evolve to a greater sphere of living.

- True glory is the reward of humble service.

Humility is an essential ingredient for growth. It prevents arguments, ends our need to be defensive, and crowns us with honor. It breeds respect, attracts admiration, and cultivates friendships. Humility helps us remember that we have a great deal to learn. The wisest recognize that they actually know very little. No matter how much we know, when compared with the magnificent universe we live in, our knowledge is only a pebble in the eternal stream of consciousness.

A wise, elderly woman lived a few blocks from me when I lived in a suburb of Houston. I never knew her real name, but all the neighborhood kids called her Nanny. She removed splinters, bandaged scraped knees, told delightful stories, and made the best oatmeal-raisin cookies I've ever tasted. But no matter how much any of us thanked her for her good deeds, she just humbly smiled, looked up at the sky, and said, "Thank God." She was so grateful and humble that she became a legend of sorts. Everyone seemed to know her, we all sang her praises, and she received more gifts each month than some people receive in several years.

Link Your Daily Deeds with Your Purpose

If you do a good job for others,
you heal yourself at the same time,
because a dose of joy is a spiritual cure.
It transcends all barriers.
— Ed Sullivan

- Service performed with gratitude is a direct expression of unconditional love.

- You live in love to the exact extent that you express love.

- To manifest your inspired dreams, help others manifest theirs.

- When you link your daily deeds with your inspired purpose, your magnetism grows and your success soars.

When you help others achieve their goals and reap rewards, you achieve an inner peace of mind that acts as a magnetic enthusiasm to attract your heartfelt desires. When you link your daily acts of service with your inspired purpose in life, your magnetism increases, and your sphere of influence grows. This magnetism is in direct proportion to how grateful you are for the opportunity to serve others, and how clearly you see that helping others serves your ultimate purpose in life. The more you're motivated by your heart, the more you receive for your inspired service.

Giving with the intention to receive is a different form of giving—more like trading or bartering. This type of giving has its place, too, but it's not the highest form of giving and therefore doesn't reap the highest rewards. Just remember that inspired action and service to others produces a high vibration of energy and magnetism, and action and service to the universe produces radiant energy and compelling magnetism.

About five years ago, a young woman by the name of Anne attended The Breakthrough Experience. During those two days, Anne discovered that all of her most inspiring experiences were preparing her for her ultimate mission and purpose in life.

She said, "I've done so many different things that they just seemed like a bunch of unrelated events. But now I can see a clear pattern running through my entire life. I can't believe I never saw this before!" She recounted her experiences with public speaking, her education in philosophy and interpersonal communications, and her firm belief that everyone has something unique to offer the world. "My mission in life is to serve others by teaching and writing about the power of unconditional love and helping other people discover their own brilliance," Anne said.

She was very clear and inspired about her mission. Turning to me, she asked, "How do I make the transition from public relations to my own teaching and writing business?" I helped Anne look at each activity she performed in public relations and find a few ways that each one was helping prepare her for her new business. She realized a deeper level of gratitude for her job, refined her vision of her life's mission, and had an abundance of inspired ideas.

She later told me that the more she helped other people see their own magnificence, the more support she received to open her new business. Today, Anne's teaching and writing helps people find their inspiration and follow their heartfelt dreams.

The Truth Is . . .

No person was ever honored for what he received.
Honor has been the reward for what he gave.
— Calvin Coolidge

- Loving acts of service attract abundance and recognition.

- When you humbly turn the credit you receive over to others, your magnetism grows.

- Linking your inspired acts of service to your ultimate purpose attracts energy and resources.

- You deserve as many blessings as you gratefully give to others.

Reflection

Sometimes, give your services for nothing.
— Hippocrates

1. Recall a time when you helped someone achieve his or her goal, and as a result, you received help from them or others to achieve your goal.

2. Think of a situation when—just as you were patting yourself on the back with pride—the rug was pulled out from under you.

3. Recall an event or situation when you did a wonderful job or made a remarkable accomplishment, but remained humble about your own performance and turned the praise you received over to others. Close your eyes and relive the feeling of warmth and the glow of love that you felt inside your heart at that moment.

4. Be thankful for your opportunity to serve others.

Realizations

No act of kindness, no matter how small, is ever wasted.
— Aesop

1. List three achievements that you're proud of
    accomplishing.

2. For each of the achievements you listed, write five
    ways that you received help from others.

3. List the three most recent acts of service you have
    performed. Then write five ways that these acts of
    love helped you fulfill your own inspired dreams.

Affirmations

- *I am grateful for my opportunities to help others
  fulfill their inspired dreams.*

- *I am humble about my accomplishments and give
  the praise to others.*

- *I link my inspired acts of service to my ultimate
  purpose.*

- *I serve the inspirations of my heart and soul and am
  rewarded with unconditional love.*

Chapter 16

Infatuation Leads to Resentment

*Infatuation is when you put a guy
on the tallest pedestal you can build,
and two months later you wish he'd jump.*
— New York graffiti

Are You Busy Building Pedestals?

Generally, the people who build the tallest pedestals experience the deepest resentment down the road, and the bigger the infatuation, the harder it falls. When you see a person, a situation, an object, or a possession as all good, you're in a temporary state of infatuation and illusion. In other words . . . *you're kidding yourself!* The reality of this universe is dualistic, so for every perceived positive, there's a perceived negative to balance the scales. We can keep our eyes and hearts open and see both sides of the people, events, and things in our lives, or we can hang from our imaginary pedestals until they begin to disintegrate and come tumbling down.

Ironically, we're the ones creating the illusions that

we eventually resent. But we don't have to go around in this illusory circle. As soon as we recognize them, we can balance our illusions and infatuations, and in this way we can learn to love the truth.

One reason that people latch on to unbalanced illusions is that they're looking for unrealistic sources of satisfaction outside of themselves. They want to believe that their new job, their favorite car, or the dream house they're building is going to bring them happiness. They become elated about their infatuations and create countless unrealistic expectations. Then, as they begin to discover aspects of the job, car, or house that they don't like, they often experience a letdown. The same principle holds true for relationships. When people are elated and infatuated, they're prime candidates for emotional heartache.

A young woman named Charlene, who worked in the sales office of a four-star Texas hotel, assisted my office staff with planning a number of personal success programs that we presented in the hotel. Charlene and I had developed a friendly rapport, and one day when I was checking into that hotel, she approached me and exclaimed, "Oh, Dr. Demartini, I've met the most wonderful man! He's perfect! He's cute, and he's smart! He has a great job, and he's really nice, and he loves kids, and dogs . . ."

Charlene was so elated and infatuated that she could hardly contain her emotional energy. I knew that unless she began balancing her perceptions and seeing the whole picture, she was heading for disappointment, so I said, "Well, that's great, Charlene! Now, tell me what you *don't* like about him."

She put her hands on her hips and said, "Dr. Demartini, do you always have to be so sensible? I'm telling you, this guy is for real!"

"Yes," I said, "and that's why you'd be wise to see and acknowledge the other side of him." She smiled and said that she'd think about it.

We didn't discuss it again until I returned to that hotel, about three months later. This time Charlene thanked me: "You know, I'm glad you encouraged me to take an honest look at Todd. I wanted him to be my knight in shining armor and convinced myself that he was."

Charlene told me that she and Todd were no longer dating. "Thank goodness you encouraged me to take a closer look at the big picture. I didn't look very closely, but I did realize that Todd wasn't the only man on Earth. And it's a good thing, because three weeks after I saw you, he left town with a country singer."

Infatuation Is Based on a Lopsided Perception

Infatuation is when you think he's as sexy as Robert Redford, as smart as Henry Kissinger, as noble as Ralph Nader, as funny as Woody Allen, and as athletic as Jimmy Connors. Love is when you realize that he's as sexy as Woody Allen, as funny as Ralph Nader, as athletic as Henry Kissinger, and nothing like Robert Redford—but you'll take him anyway.
— Judith Viorst

- If you have a one-sided view of anything, it can ruin your life.

- The feeling or belief that you must have something or someone is a sign that you're infatuated.

- When your perception of a situation or person is all good, your perception is lopsided.

- The degree or intensity of the infatuation determines the degree or intensity of the resentment that may follow.

A few years ago, after speaking to a group of Mary Kay Cosmetics directors and beauty consultants in San Diego, I had the opportunity to consult privately with some of them. When one young woman asked if I thought that she should marry the man she was dating, I asked her to tell me about him. She said, "Dr. Demartini, this guy is flawless. He's everything I've ever wanted. I love everything about him."

Her description was too lopsided to be true. I knew that no one could live up to the image she described, and the unrealistic expectations she had now would lead to some degree of resentment later. I told her that I didn't think she would be wise to marry him at this stage in their relationship.

"Well, what do you think I should do?" she asked.

I asked her to list all his good character traits. Quickly she listed 60 or more good traits. Next, I asked her to list beside these positive traits all the traits she considered bad or negative.

Immediately she became angry and defensive. "If he had as many bad traits as good, I wouldn't be in love with him!" she said in a huff.

I explained that I thought her description of him was unrealistic, and that if she didn't balance her perceptions and see the big picture now, she would certainly be awakened to the reality once they were married.

I explained that when we see the complete person—both

the things we like and those we don't—we have a greater chance of experiencing a more fulfilling relationship.

She agreed to try to balance the list of her perceived positives and negatives. It took some time, but she continued digging and pushing herself until she had listed as many negatives as she had positives. When she reviewed what she had written, her eyes filled with tears.

"I didn't want to look at any of the things that I thought I might not like about him." she said. "I thought it would be better just to ignore those things. But now that they're all written down and in the open, I have a better idea of who he really is."

Next, I asked her to go back to the "good" list she'd made, and one by one, look inside herself to find the same character traits that she admired and appreciated in him. As she completed this part of the exercise, she began to realize that she didn't "need" her boyfriend as much as she had imagined originally. She began to understand that the traits he had, which she thought she was lacking, she actually had after all. She got over her feeling of infatuation codependence with him, and by doing so, she overcame the blocks that stood in the way of balanced, unconditional love.

Upon reaching this level of understanding and gratitude, tears streamed down her face. "I now know that I don't need him," she said, "and I know there are things about him that I don't like, but the most amazing thing is that I know I truly love him."

Resentment Sets in When Expectations Aren't Met

Wisdom comes by disillusionment.
— George Santayana

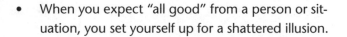

- When you expect "all good" from a person or situation, you set yourself up for a shattered illusion.

- When you're resentful, you create a wall around yourself that repels inspiration and blocks your ability to feel the unconditional love in your heart and soul.

- Finding the benefits in the people and situations that you resent balances your lopsided perceptions and gives you another opportunity to express unconditional love and gratitude for what is, as it is.

- Infatuation—*not* unconditional love—is the opposite of hate, and the very state into which so many fall.

Resentment tends to set in when the expectations you have for someone or some occasion aren't met. When you are resentful, you believe there are more negatives than positives. But the reality is that resentments, just like infatuations, are based on misjudgments. When you balance your perceptions and see the person or event in a truthful light, you rise above infatuation and resentment to experience unconditional love.

I recently consulted with a young man named Ken who was feeling very resentful toward his wife, Lona. In our first appointment Ken said, "I don't know what happened. She was my dream come true when we were dating, and now she's my worst nightmare!"

I asked Ken to tell me more about his perception of Lona when they were dating, and I also asked him what he expected from her as his wife. As we talked, it became evident that what Ken thought was okay for his girlfriend, was not okay for his wife. He held a number of unspoken expectations about how he wanted Lona to act and treat him, and he was resentful that she wasn't fulfilling his wishes.

I took Ken through The Demartini Method to help him bring his perceptions back into balance and to see the magnificence of what he was actually experiencing. When he completed the Method, he wrote a thank-you letter to Lona expressing his gratitude for her being exactly as she is. He realized that the resentment he'd been feeling, and the heartache he was experiencing, were based entirely on his own misperceptions and his hidden and unrealistic expectations.

The Truth Is . . .

It is not love, but lack of love, which is blind.
— Glenway Westcott

- When you see only what you perceive to be positive in a person, thing, or event, you're infatuated.

- Basing expectations on illusions creates unrealistic expectations.

- Resentment and disappointment often result from infatuation and illusion.

- When you balance your perceptions and appreciate the perfection of the truth, you experience unconditional love, and you heal.

Reflections

The truth shall set you free.
— John 8:32

1. Recall your most recent infatuation with a person, thing, or event.

2. Play back your mental tape of what you said and thought about that person, thing, or event during the infatuation stage.

3. Now, play back your mental tape of what you said and thought about the same person, thing, or event once you realized that they, or it, had as many negatives as positives.

4. Ask yourself what outcome you originally expected from the person, thing, or event.

Realizations

The great enemy of truth is very often not the lie—deliberate, contrived, and dishonest—but the myth persistent—persuasive, and unrealistic.
— John F. Kennedy

1. Write the name of the person, thing, or event with whom or which you're most infatuated right now.

2. List ten character traits or characteristics that you like and ten you don't like about the object of your infatuation.

3. Now, review the ten characteristics or traits you like. Circle the one you believe that you or your life lacks the most.

4. List three times when you demonstrated the character trait or possessed the characteristic that you think you lack.

Affirmations

- *I am balancing my perceptions so I can see, appreciate, and love the truth.*

- *I am grateful for my ability to acknowledge the balance in all I experience.*

- *I am dissolving my illusions and turning my resentment into love.*

- *I welcome the grace and healing of my heart and soul's unconditional love.*

Chapter 17

Everyone Is Your Mirror

A loving person lives in a loving world.
A hostile person lives in a hostile world.
Everyone you meet is your mirror.
— Ken Keyes, Jr.

Who's Running Your Life?

Chances are, it's not always you! We have a funny way of letting people with whom we're infatuated, and those toward whom we're angry, dominate our thoughts and conversation, and sometimes even make us sick. But once we see that we personally have all those characteristics that we like or dislike in others, we have the power to run our own lives!

It doesn't take much observation to notice that we get caught up in our feelings and opinions about other people. Most of us spend a good bit of time complaining about certain people while singing the praises of others. We tend to dislike those who display the character traits we refuse to acknowledge and love in ourselves, and we generally like the people who reflect the traits we respect and value in ourselves.

You don't have to let other people run your life. By acknowledging that what you see in others is a reflection of yourself, you unfold the potential to be set free. As soon as you can see where you, at some time, have displayed the character traits you dislike in others, you begin to see how those qualities benefit you. Every trait—whether you like it or dislike it—serves a purpose. On the other hand, once you recall a time when you displayed the same traits that you like and admire in others, you realize that you also have them in yourself, and they serve a purpose, too!

When I teach the concept of others being our mirror, I often think about a young man who was approaching his first wedding anniversary. Brian phoned me in exasperation about the arguments that he and his wife had been having. He said that his wife Carol was great and that they were very compatible, but he didn't like Carol's best friend, Sandy. Carol was angry because Brian rarely agreed to socialize with Sandy and her husband, and he wasn't fond of Sandy's frequent visits.

"You'd think since Carol and I are so much alike, I'd get along with her best friend, but so many things about Sandy really get on my nerves," Brian said. I explained that, at one time or another, we all display each of the many human personality traits—the ones we like as well as the ones we dislike. Some of us may temporarily develop and express certain traits more than others, but essentially we all have the full palette, so everyone we meet is our mirror. To illustrate this principle, I asked Brian to tell me three qualities he liked about Carol that he also liked about himself. He quickly responded, "She has a lot of energy, she's smart, and she's funny."

Next I asked him to think about Sandy and tell me three characteristics he didn't like about her that he also didn't like about himself. This time his response took longer. "I can't think of anything," he said. I encouraged him to think harder and he said, "Okay, she's impatient, and I'm impatient, too." "Great," I said. "How about two more?"

After a moment Brian said, "She always has to be the first one to go to a new or trendy place, and then she always comes over to gloat about it!" When I asked if he also liked to be the first to experience new places, he said that he enjoyed going to new restaurants, shops, and night clubs to "get the scoop" on them, but he denied any form of gloating.

"Do you ever tell anyone about your discoveries or adventures?" I asked.

"Well, yeah, I usually tell my brother-in-law Bob. He's a high roller for a big corporation and he prides himself on being in the know about all the hot spots in the city. It really throws him when I casually mention having a fabulous evening at a place he's never heard of! Hey, but that's not really gloating, is it?"

I congratulated him on thinking of two more things— wanting to be the first and enjoying the opportunity to brag a little.

"Okay, so Sandy and I have a few things in common. How does that solve my problem?" Brian asked.

I explained to Brian that the only characteristics we see in other people are ones we have in ourselves. I suggested that Carol reflects many of the traits he likes about himself, while Sandy reflects traits he dislikes about himself. "When you notice Sandy doing something you don't like, ask yourself when and where in your own life you've done the same thing," I suggested. "Then, look at those times and see how they actually benefited someone."

Brian was silent for a moment, then said, "So I guess I could try to find ways that Sandy is somehow benefiting me." Then, laughing, he added, "Okay, but if anyone else would have said Sandy's benefiting me, I'd have denied it to the end!"

The People with Whom You Interact Show You Who You Are and Ultimately Provide You with an Opportunity to Love Yourself

The people we are in relationship with are always a mirror, reflecting our own beliefs and simultaneously we are mirrors reflecting their beliefs. So relationship is one of the most powerful tools for growth. . . . If we look honestly at our relationships we can see so much about how we have created them.
— Shakti Gawain

- If you appreciate a trait in someone else, you can find it in yourself.

- If you admire someone for their creative talent, you're creative—although you may not yet have discovered or acknowledged your own abilities.

- If you enjoy someone else's company because they're funny, you possess an equally good sense of humor.

Human nature causes us to seek the company of people who have character traits we like about ourselves. It's self-affirming. When we meet someone with whom we bond, we say things like "we're so much alike." But when we say this, we're probably looking at the "likable" parts of that person.

Sometimes you value a trait or an ability that someone else has because you think that you don't have it yourself. But if you can see it and appreciate it in someone else, you have it in yourself. We have relationships with people who reflect who we are. The purpose of marriage and relationships isn't just so-called happiness, as some might imagine. It's self-discovery. We learn about ourselves by interacting with our mates, our friends, our associates, and everyone we encounter.

The people who irritate us the most are the ones we might want to observe the most. They're reflecting back to us those things about ourselves that we haven't learned to feel grateful for and love. Since our mission is to discover what we don't love and learn to love it, the people who get on our nerves most are among our greatest teachers!

A year ago, a young man named Steven attended one of my programs called Prophecy. His shirt had a beautiful, intricate rose painted on the front. When Nancy, one of the women in the program, complimented him on it and asked him where he bought such a magnificent piece of art, he began to blush. Almost apologetically, he explained that he used an airbrush to paint the rose himself.

"You're an artist!" the woman exclaimed.

Looking even more uncomfortable, Steven said, "Oh no, I'm not an artist. I love great artwork, and I wish I had the talent to create it, but I'm far from an artist."

Nancy and Steven continued to debate this issue until I spoke up and explained that we can't appreciate a talent in someone else that we don't have within ourselves. When Nancy enthusiastically agreed, I asked her how she expressed her artistry. She denied having any artistry or creativity whatsoever. I restated the principle that she couldn't appreciate Steven's creativity if she didn't have it within herself as well. After some discussion, Nancy acknowledged that she has a unique artistic flair for interior decorating.

Just because you're not currently an expert at something doesn't mean you don't possess what it takes to become one! Every expert begins as an amateur. Today Steven is using his airbrush to create beautiful pictures, and he's also pursuing his skills in photography again. He admits that recognizing the artist within was the most enlightening and most difficult part of developing his own talent. He would love to create fine artwork someday that's good enough to hang in galleries and museums, and he knows he's on his way to achieving his goal.

At times it can be difficult to see that we have the qualities and talents we admire in other people. But it can be even more of a challenge to accept that we also possess the traits we don't like in others.

Whatever You See in Others Is a Reflection of You— Whether You Like It or Not!

> *Basically my wife was immature.*
> *I'd be at home in the bath and*
> *she'd come in and sink my boats.*
> *— Woody Allen*

- You can only see things in others that exist in
  yourself.

- If you're bothered by someone who you think is
  rude, then you also have the capacity to be rude.

- When you feel uncomfortable or judgmental
  about someone else's actions or behavior, it's
  because they remind you of what you don't
  yet love about yourself.

- You love yourself as much as you love others; you
  love others as much as you love yourself.

Several months ago, Martha came into my office for
a consultation. She told me that her father had died and
her mother was getting to a point where she could no
longer take care of herself. She felt that she should invite
her mother to come live with her family, but the thought
of it made her cringe.

Martha began talking about her mother's faults at
length, and I finally asked her to list the ten things she liked
least about her mother and to circle the one she disliked
the most. Once her list was complete, I noticed she had
circled know-it-all.

"Give me an example of how your mother is a know-it-
all," I said.

"There are a million examples," Martha said. "Just last
week she called me to ask how my doctor's visit went. I told
her my blood pressure was high, and she went on and on
about how I should live, what I should and shouldn't eat,
and how I would be better off if I took her advice!"

"Was it wise advice?" I asked.

Martha admitted that some of it was exactly as the doctor ordered, but she added, "I'm 34 years old, and there's nothing my mother can tell me that I don't already know!"

I allowed her comment to linger in the stillness of the room. Finally, I said, "So your mother bothers you because she's a know-it-all, and you already know everything."

"That's exactly right," she said.

"Does that mean that you're a know-it-all, too?" I asked.

The truth sets us free, but it usually startles us or makes us angry first! Martha and her mother still have what they imagine are their differences, but Martha realized there's truth in the statement that what we dislike in others, we haven't learned to love in ourselves. She has been learning a great deal about herself since her mother moved in, and while she isn't fond of some of her new awareness, she's grateful to have such an accurate mirror.

Our human mirrors always reflect our own reality. But at least in the short run, it's easier to judge and criticize others than it is to take an honest, objective look at ourselves. In the long run, though, we must learn about ourselves through others' reflections in order to grow and develop. Sometimes, however, our pain and discomfort put a wall between us and the people we don't like. The irony is that often the more we dislike and criticize a character trait in someone else, the more of it we have within ourselves.

I recently did some work with a man named Paul, whose daughter Beth was killed by a drunk driver. Paul blamed the drunk driver, he blamed himself for letting Beth borrow the car, and he even blamed God. He was angry, and he wanted revenge. He said that he wasn't interested in pursuing justice, because justice could never bring back his daughter. I asked how revenge could bring back his daughter. Paul said that he knew it couldn't, but he wanted to make the man who killed his daughter feel as miserable as he felt.

As we discussed the situation, Paul said the act of killing someone was the worst act a person could commit, and he self-righteously claimed he never did anything that could jeopardize someone else's life.

"Have you ever driven after you've had a few drinks?" I asked.

"Well, yes," he said, " but I wasn't drunk!"

"Do you know that even one alcoholic drink begins to impair your reflexes?" I asked.

"One drink barely impairs my reflexes! I've driven perfectly well even after having two or three drinks. The man who killed my daughter was so drunk he could barely walk!"

"But couldn't driving after two or three drinks impair your reflexes and judgment enough to put someone else's life in jeopardy?" I asked.

He began to get angry. He stood up and said, "I've never driven a car when I was too drunk to walk a straight line! I'm nothing like the man who murdered Beth."

Over the next hour, Paul realized that he had, in fact, made many choices in his life that could have jeopardized someone else's life. He had driven his car and operated heavy machinery after taking a prescription drug that causes drowsiness and is labeled with a warning not to drive or operate equipment when taking the drug. He also remembered drinking and driving when he was pledging a college fraternity. As part of his initiation, he drank a pint of vodka, then drove across town to a party where he drank several beers before driving home. He admitted that he sometimes broke the speed limit, and that several times when driving home late at night, he had begun to fall asleep at the wheel before pulling over.

By the end of our session, Paul knew that he had more in common with the drunk driver than he had ever imagined. He said that he felt humbled by his own memories and sad that he could have jeopardized lives, including his own.

I wanted Paul to see how his own actions, even the memories he felt sad about, served him in some way and also helped someone else in some way. So I asked him to look at these memories and find at least one way that each of his actions helped him and someone else. He resisted this instruction, saying he couldn't believe that his choice to drive when he had been drinking or was exhausted could have helped him or anyone else at all, so I asked him to consider how those choices are helping him now.

He was silent for a moment, and then he began to cry. "I guess I never really appreciated my own life. I was willing to take risks because I didn't realize what a gift it is to be alive. But now I'll be more thoughtful about my own driving decisions, and I'm sure that will help me and help the other people on the road, too," Paul said.

He also began to see how Beth's death had awakened his love for his other family members and his friends. "Beth has given me a new chance at my own life," Paul said, "a chance to appreciate what I have, and a chance to learn to love myself and others. I've had such a closed heart, but now I can feel that it's open."

The Truth Is . . .

There is hope for us all when we can look in
the mirror and laugh at what we see.
— Anonymous

- Life's many mirrors are your teachers and healers.

- Whatever you can see clearly and in balance no longer controls or disrupts your mind or body.

- You love yourself as much as you love others.

- You love others as much as you love yourself.

- Whatever you see in someone else—whether you think it's good or bad—you have within yourself.

- Whatever you admire in someone else, you have within yourself.

- Whatever you dislike in someone else, you have within yourself.

- You can learn to appreciate and love whatever you have within yourself. This is one of the secrets of healing.

- Life is like a movie screen: It reflects what you project.

Reflections

We often choose a friend as we do a mistress;
for no particular excellence in themselves,
but merely from some circumstance that flatters our self-love.
— William Hazlitt

1. Think of three things that you've admired in someone else and later went on to do or accomplish yourself.

2. Think of something you swore you'd never do, but *have* done.

3. Think of three compliments you've paid to other people that other people have also paid to you.

4. Think of three things for which you have criticized other people, and for which others have also criticized you.

Realizations

Self-reflection is the school of wisdom.
— Baltasar Gracián y Morales

1. Write three character traits that you admire in other people.

2. Write three character traits that you dislike in other people.

3. Write three specific examples of times you've exhibited each of the character traits you admire.

4. Write three specific examples of times you've exhibited each of the character traits you dislike.

Affirmations

- *Whatever I see in others I have within myself.*

- *Whatever I see in others helps me love myself.*

- *Whatever I see in others helps me heal myself.*

- *I am loving my reflections as my greatest teachers.*

- *I am grateful for life's many mirrors.*

Chapter 18

Whatever You Say to Others, You're Saying to Yourself

No matter what we talk about, we're talking about ourselves.
— Anonymous

What Are You Talking About?

People tend to talk about what interests them most. If they like sports, they talk about sports; they talk about politics if they like politics; and if they're interested in the details of other people's lives, they talk about people. Regardless of the topic of conversation, however, the statements people make are reflections of what they're telling themselves or things they believe they need to hear. For example, if two people are about to cross a narrow ledge on the side of a tall mountain, the one who says, "Whatever you do, don't look down," is most assuredly talking to him- or herself.

After studying human language and its origins for years, modern linguists have determined that our verbal expression has evolved from our internal thoughts and inner dialogue. It appears that the original intent of language was more to help us understand ourselves than just to communicate with others. The words you use, the advice you give, and the topics you select are all messages that are meant for you as well. So if you're healing an illness, your own messages can give you valuable insight into some of your perceptions.

A demonstration of this principle occurred at one of my recent personal success programs called Empyreance. During the ten-day course, I heard a man named Don tell three people in the program that they had the skills to start their own successful businesses. After the third time, I asked him what business he wanted to start.

He looked a bit surprised and said, "Well, I'm already an engineer."

I smiled and asked again, "What business would you love to start, Don?"

He was silent for a minute, then said, "I'd really like to open my own restaurant."

Each time Don told someone they could succeed in business, he was also telling himself. So when you listen to what you're saying, you learn what you want to hear. And while this knowledge may be humbling, it can also be a gateway to a deeper level of understanding and love.

Just Listen to Yourself

If nobody ever said anything unless he knew what he was talking about, a ghastly hush would descend upon the earth.
— Alan Herbert

- The words you use are clues to your state of mind.

- When you think a character trait is lacking in someone else, you may fear it's lacking in you.

- Listen to what you complain about and you'll hear your own justifications and rationalizations.

- When you hear yourself say "always" or "never," know that it's probably a lie.

When you're making a lot of statements like: "I have to do this," and "I should do that," you're buying into the illusion that other people and circumstances are controlling your life. When you hear yourself say things like: "I choose to do this," and "I love to do that," you're hearing the voice of self-fulfillment, which grows out of your inner knowledge that you're in control of your life. But most people oscillate between following their inner voices of true inspiration and following the outer voices of others' desperation. Acting out of desperation is often caused by thinking something is lacking from your life.

If you want to find out what you think you don't have, listen to what you think and say others don't have. For example, if you place a high value on being efficient and you're not as efficient as you want to be, you may hear yourself complain of others' inefficiency.

In general, whatever you complain about regarding someone else represents a part of you that you haven't seen in balance and learned to love. If you complain about someone being a "big fat liar," you've no doubt told a few big fat lies of your own, but when you balance your perceptions of the lies you've told and appreciate the benefits of the lessons you've learned, you no longer have such strong negative feelings about other people's lies. The more you look at the justifications and rationalizations in your own lies, the more clearly you can see what's stopping you and find your way around it.

Two of the easiest keys to recognizing that you're lying are the words *always* and *never.* Whenever you use one or the other word, it's generally part of a lie, and the more strongly you claim that you'll never do something, the sooner you may find yourself doing it.

Just the other day, as I was admiring a ring in a San Diego jewelry store, I heard a familiar voice behind me and turned to see Chris, one of my clients. He smiled from ear to ear as he told me that he was selecting an engagement ring for his girlfriend, Joyce. Upon congratulating him, he asked, "Do you remember what you told me that last time I saw you?"

I thought for a moment and recalled that the last time I talked to Chris, he vowed that he'd never fall in love again! Before I could answer, Chris said, "You told me that the stronger I swore that I'd never fall in love again, the sooner I'd probably do it, and you were right! I met Joyce a month after I swore off women!"

Pay Attention to Your Own Advice

> *Practice yourself what you preach.*
> — Titus Maccius Plautus

- When you offer guidance to someone, listen for the pearls of wisdom you're sharing with yourself.

- Where you see room for improvement in someone else, you see room for improvement in yourself.

- The direction you tell others to go may be the direction you most want to go.

- When you understand and appreciate that you're an expression of the perfection of the universe, you become speechless with unconditional love.

I once asked a seven-year-old boy named Nick what he thought "practice what you preach" meant. He said it meant don't tell somebody to do something unless you do it yourself. As an example, he said, "I shouldn't tell my sister to put her toys away unless I put my own toys away." Nick certainly grasped the basic aspect of this statement. But what he didn't yet understand is that what we preach is what we believe we need to hear. That's why our advice to others is often our advice to ourselves. It makes sense that our opinions are more useful and valid for us than for others, because they're based on our own unique life experiences.

Several years ago, a single mother named Tami came to me for help coping with her 15-year-old daughter, Kristen. Tami said that no matter what she did, she couldn't convince her daughter to put more time into her studies. I asked Tami if Kristen was failing any of her classes. "Why would you think she was failing?" asked Tami. "She's not getting all A's and B's, but she isn't failing either!" she assured me.

As we continued talking, Tami told me that she was afraid if her daughter didn't keep her grades up, she wouldn't be accepted into college. "She has to work hard and keep her priorities straight," she said.

As I listened to Tami, I realized the anxiety she felt about her daughter's grades was a reflection of her own fear of rejection. I asked Tami if she went to college and she looked down at the ground and said, "No, but someday I will." Tami discovered that her desire to attend college was much greater than she had been admitting to herself. Every time she encouraged Kristen to study and earn good grades, she was wishing that she had listened to her own mother's advice when she was in high school. Tami acknowledged that pressuring Kristen over the past few years hadn't seemed to make a difference in her grades. She agreed to start taking her own advice.

Instead of standing over Kristen every night, making sure she completed her studies, Tami did some studying of her own. She enrolled in a course to help her prepare for her college entrance exam, and she decided to start visiting colleges in the area.

About six months later, Tami said, "I did great on my entrance exams, and I'm deciding between two different colleges." I told Tami that I thought her accomplishment was great, and I asked her how Kristen was doing. "That's the weirdest part of all this," she said. "As soon as I stopped riding her about studying, I noticed she was working on her own. And last quarter, she made the honor roll!"

The Truth Is . . .

It does not require many words to speak the truth.
— Inmuttooyahlatlat (Chief Joseph)

- You often say out loud what you need to hear most softly in your heart.

- Your words reflect the way you see yourself and your world.

- When you give advice to others, it applies to your own life somewhere or somehow.

- Your complaints are about the aspects of your life that you have yet to learn to appreciate and love.

Reflections

He gave man speech, and speech created thought,
Which is the measure of the universe.
— Percy Bysshe Shelley

1. Replay the conversations you've had today and notice whether you said "have to" and "should" more than "choose to" and "love."

2. Make a commitment to start paying close attention to what you're saying.

3. Recall the last time you swore that you'd never do a particular thing.

4. Recall how much time passed before you did it.

Realizations

Learn to be silent. Let your quiet mind listen and absorb.
— Pythagoras

1. If you were asked to share three pieces of wise advice with others, what would they be? Write them down.

2. Look for a way that you can apply to your own life each piece of advice you wrote, and write it down as well.

3. Think of your greatest complaint about other people in general—or about someone in particular—and write it out.

4. Now list three ways you have demonstrated this same action in one of the seven areas of your life (social, family, vocational, financial, physical, mental, or spiritual).

Affirmations

- *I listen for the hidden wisdom in my words to others.*

- *When I hear myself complaining, I ask myself what I am trying to balance and love.*

- *I am changing my life by changing my words. I am healing my body by loving myself.*

- *I am healing my life by loving the perfection in the universe.*

Chapter 19

Whatever You Think You Don't Have, You Want the Most

The grass looks greener on the opposite side of the fence.
— Traditional proverb

What Do You Think You're Missing?

Many people think their lives are lacking something, and in most cases, they put the highest value on whatever it is they believe is missing most. If they don't have a partner, they may place the greatest value on having one. If they lack the quality of health they want, they probably place the most value on healing. If it's money they want most, they may place the highest value on earning more; or if they believe they lack a good job, finding a new one will have the highest value.

In other words, the voids you perceive to be greatest become your greatest values. But your ultimate sense of fulfillment isn't in events, material possessions, jobs, or even other people. It's in you. And the truth is, anything you can see outside yourself, you already have within. When you value a character trait in someone else, know that you already have that trait within yourself. The same principle holds true for possessions. It's not really the possession that you want, it's what the possession means or represents to you, and whatever it represents, you're sure to have in some form in your life already.

In one of my personal success programs, a woman named Paula was convinced that her life would be changed miraculously if she had an automatic dishwasher. She said that she desperately needed more personal time, and a dishwasher could solve her problems and make a big difference in her life. I suggested to Paula that she balance the infatuation she had with the concept of owning a dishwasher and reminded her that when we fill one perceived void, we discover another.

The interesting thing is that just a few weeks ago I received a letter from Paula. She said, "You were right when you said that as soon as we fill one void, the next one appears! After I got the dishwasher and had more leisure time, I realized how out of shape I was. So my new highest value is to get back into shape!" She enclosed a photograph of herself standing next to a home-fitness machine; the note on the back read: *My love affair with the Maytag has cooled, and my new "void come true" is this gorgeous bodybuilder!*

The Greater the Void, the Greater the Value

To have a grievance is to have a purpose in life.
— Eric Hoffer

- Whatever you think you're missing is what you want the most.

- You actually have every character trait, but you may not recognize it yet.

- When your highest-priority void is filled, the next void in line moves up to become your highest priority.

- The principle you value most is often one that you didn't see demonstrated to you at an earlier stage of your life.

The old adage that the grass is always greener on the other side of the fence is just another variation of the principle that you seek whatever you think you lack. For example, you may place a high value on people who are funny because you love to laugh, but since you can sense and appreciate the humor outside yourself, you have an unrecognized humor within yourself as well.

Voids in our lives can serve as some of our best chauffeurs through life. We're driven to fill our highest-priority void, even though we know another one will pop up to replace it. Often, the principles we value most have such importance for us because we feel that they are, or have been, missing from our own lives.

On a flight from Manhattan to North Carolina, I sat next to a woman named Mary who was a law-enforcement officer. I asked what motivated her to pursue a career in law enforcement and she lightheartedly said, "Well, somebody's gotta uphold the law."

I knew there was more to it than that, so I asked, "Who

'broke the law' in your life?" Mary said there were no lawbreakers in her life except the ones she handcuffed and hauled off to jail.

"Not even when you were younger? Before you decided to be a police officer?" I asked.

Shrugging her shoulders she claimed that she couldn't think of any. As we continued talking, she shared that most of her cases dealt with domestic violence. "You wouldn't believe all the people who end up in emergency rooms every day because of domestic violence," she told me. As she described a recent case, her voice became louder and filled with emotion. "You can't believe some of the injuries I've seen," she said, with fire in her eyes. I then knew that Mary had either experienced or witnessed domestic violence at some point in her life.

"Mary, how old were you the first time you experienced domestic violence?" I asked.

Her first reaction was surprise, then her eyes filled with tears. "My father beat my mom so hard that I was sure he'd kill her," she said. "In those days the police didn't help much. They didn't want to interfere in what they called 'family affairs.'" Mary was silent for a moment, then she looked up at me and smiled. "Hey, I guess there *was* a 'lawbreaker' in my life." Mary's early belief that her mother was missing protection from the legal system led her to fill that void by becoming a police officer and working with people involved with domestic violence.

What's Missing Can Be Motivating

Every man believes that he has greater possibility.
— Ralph Waldo Emerson

- Your illusive perception that something is missing can be one of your greatest motivators.

- What you feel you're missing is often what you value most.

- A perceived void is a gift to help you learn another lesson of unconditional love.

- Nothing is really missing.

We can feel sorry for ourselves over what we think is missing in our lives, or we can use what we think we lack to motivate us to new achievements. Either way, nothing is actually missing; it's only in an unrecognized form. Whatever we feel is missing provides us with an opportunity to learn another lesson in the balance of unconditional love.

I consulted with a woman named Theresa who told me, "When I was single, I thought that I needed to be in love, to be happy. Now I'm in love, and I'm still not happy." She explained that a few years before, her biggest priority had been to find her soul mate. She was sure that if she could meet the right guy, the void in her life would be filled. She registered with several dating services and met one man after another. After several months of this routine, she met Matt, whom she had been dating for the past six months.

Now, however, Theresa was experiencing a new void in her life: "I'm bored with my job; it's just not fulfilling. I think that if I can get a job that makes a difference, I'll be a lot happier. Or maybe I should have a baby. Maybe that would make me happy."

I explained to Theresa that I believed her search for happiness was leading her on a wild-goose chase. I encouraged her to look inside her heart for the mission or purpose that she would love to pursue and let that be her true beacon and guide in life. I said, "You'll always experience happiness and sadness, Theresa, but if you work toward your inspired mission or purpose in life, you'll have a more steady focus, and you can embrace both sides of life more powerfully." Theresa later realized that her inspired purpose was to make a difference in the lives of children.

The Truth Is . . .

You already have everything your heart desires.
— Traditional proverb

•   Your largest voids drive your greatest values.

•   You seek what you think you don't have.

•   Nothing is missing.

•   The hierarchy of your values dictates your destiny.

Reflections

Many of us spend half our time wishing for things that we could have if we didn't spend half our time wishing.
— Alexander Woollcott

1.   Recall the last thing you bought or did because you believed it would bring fulfillment.

2. Ask yourself how your life has changed since you bought or did that.

3. Recall a childhood wish that you believe was not fulfilled when you were young.

4. In what ways have you fulfilled, or are you working toward fulfilling, that wish now?

Realizations

If you don't get what you want, it is a sign
either that you did not seriously want it,
or that you tried to bargain over the price.
— Rudyard Kipling

1. Look closely at the seven areas of your life—social, family, vocational, financial, physical, mental, and spiritual—and find whatever you believe is missing most in you or your life. Write this void on a piece of paper.

2. Write ten ways this void benefits or teaches you.

3. Think of how whatever you believe is missing actually is present in some form and area of your life. Ponder where and when you actually have what you perceived to be missing or to be a void. Don't stop until you discover it.

4. Write a thank-you letter to yourself for the lessons learned and the benefits received from this void.

Affirmations

- *I am grateful for my perception of voids because they help me identify my values.*

- *I balance my perceptions so I can see that nothing is missing.*

- *I am one with all that exists.*

- *Whatever I can sense outside of me exists within me.*

- *I am filling my body with healing energy.*

- *I am filling my life with healing love.*

Chapter 20

Whatever You Run Away from, You Run Into— Whatever You Lie about Runs Your Life

*Be not the slave of your own past, plunge into the sublime seas,
dive deep, and swim far, so you shall come back with self-respect,
with new power, with an advanced experience,
that shall explain and overlook the old.*
— Ralph Waldo Emerson

Have You Been Avoiding Yourself?

No matter how far we run, or how well we lie, we can't escape our fears, because they stem from within us. When we run from our fears, we often run right into them. That's why we encounter the same types of people, conditions, situations, and sicknesses again and again. We continue to attract lessons until we learn their messages, appreciate their blessings, and bring the dualism of our lopsided perceptions into perfect balance. Once we experience the truth behind a lesson and embrace the reality with unconditional love, we've learned that lesson and stop attracting it.

One way in which people try to run away from fears is to lie about them, but lying is motivated by fear to begin with. There are many different fears that lead us to lie, but no matter what our reason, as soon as we do it, we begin harboring a sense of guilt on a conscious or subconscious level. Over time, the fears and guilt grow in our minds and gain energy of their own. From the moment we lie, the lie begins to take over our life, and we attract and run into whatever we fear or try to run away from.

While I was waiting for a friend in a New York café, I met a man named Jim who was a youth counselor. He worked with teenagers, helping them build self-esteem and encouraging them to value their own beliefs and decisions. I thought that sounded interesting and asked him what motivated him to do this type of work. Here's what he told me:

> Well, the story begins when I was 16 years old. It was a cool October night. My mom and dad were out of town, and I took my dad's car without permission. I picked up my girlfriend, Beth, and we headed for the local drive-in restaurant that was the town hangout. Right after we pulled in, three hot rods came roaring into the parking lot, and a bunch of guys piled out of the cars. I recognized at least two of them from a fight that broke out after a football game a few weeks earlier. They were from a nearby town, and they were the kind of guys I usually tried to avoid.

Jim said it wasn't 60 seconds after silently hoping "don't come over here," that three of the guys strolled over and leaned on his car. One thing led to another, and within minutes, he had agreed to a drag race later that night. He'd never raced before, and it was about the last thing he wanted to do, but he said that he was afraid of looking like a coward.

Beth tried to talk him out of racing, but he felt like he had to do it. So later that night, after he took Beth home, Jim drove to the country road they'd agreed to race on. He wanted to get there early and practice driving up and down the road a few times before anyone else showed up.

> It was my second trial run down the road, and a deer ran in front of my car. I slammed on the brakes, hit the horn, and somehow managed to miss the deer. And then I realized that refusing to race wasn't cowardly at all. It was actually the courageous and responsible thing to do. So I gathered up all my courage and waited for the other guys to show up so I could tell them that I'd decided not to race.

He said that he was nervous and calm at the same time and the longer he waited, the better he felt about his decision, no matter what the outcome. Jim concluded:

> The irony is that no one ever came. I found out the next day that a fight had broken out in town about an hour before we were supposed to race. Four of the hot-rod guys got arrested, and everyone else went their separate ways. So I guess the lesson of the story is that we don't have to do anything to prove we have courage. We just have to be courageous enough to do—or not do—what we know is wise. And that's what I share with the teens I work with.

What You Fear Comes Near; What You Flee Follows You

*To defend one's self against fear is simply to ensure
that one will one day be conquered by it;
fears must be faced.*
— James Baldwin

- When you give your attention and energy to your fears, you become like a magnet and attract them.

- Fears are great teachers when you're willing to learn their lessons of love.

- When you run away from a person or situation, you'll run into a similar person or situation somewhere down the road.

- You can't outrun yourself.

The school of life is lovingly persistent, and it is ripe with opportunities for us to learn and grow. We attract the lessons we focus on most, and we move in the direction of our most dominant thoughts. When we focus on love and gratitude, we create an energy field that attracts more love and gratitude. When we focus on fears, we create an energy field that attracts fears—and believe it or not, that's also a benefit! It's a safeguard to make sure we receive an unlimited number of chances to learn to love.

Each time we face the underlying lesson or cause that's creating a fear, we offer ourselves an opportunity to grow to a new level of understanding. When we balance our perceptions of the benefits and drawbacks surrounding the fear, we achieve a deeper understanding that leads us out of fear and into a more enlightened state of unconditional love.

Connie, a woman who participated in The Breakthrough Experience a few years ago, shared that she was just beginning to put the pieces of her financial picture back together. She had filed for bankruptcy about two years earlier and was still very upset about it. She said, "I was always afraid that my business would go bankrupt, and when it began to happen, I just couldn't handle it." Connie explained that instead of facing the reality of her situation, she kept denying it to herself until she had no other choice but to declare bankruptcy.

As we discussed her situation, she began to see that for years she had been making business and financial decisions out of fear and desperation, rather than out of love and inspiration. Before the seminar ended, she was grateful for the blessings that had resulted from her bankruptcy.

Fear Precedes Every Lie and Guilt Follows

It is the easiest thing in the world for a man to deceive himself.
— Benjamin Franklin

- The root of a lie is fear, not dishonesty.

- Fear blocks imagination.

- Each lie plants a seed of guilt.

- Guilt blocks memory.

People don't lie because they're dishonest. They're dishonest because they're afraid of the truth. That's why fear precedes every lie. We choose to lie because we believe, that the truth may create a reaction or response we fear and want to avoid. Guilt follows every lie because our inner knowing immediately realizes that we're actively avoiding an opportunity to learn love, and we're creating another block within ourselves.

We all tell lies that end up affecting our lives in one way or another, and eventually we find out that telling the truth would have been the wiser path. I once heard a story about a man named Larry who, out of desperation, claimed to a prospective employer that he had a master's degree in business administration. He got the job, but was constantly worried that the truth might come out, and he beat himself up for telling a lie that continued to haunt him.

The longer he worked at the firm, the more the lie blossomed. Before long, he lied not only about having the degree, but also about when he received it, the school he attended, and the names of some of his professors. He had to be careful that all of his other stories fit in with that one, and after several years of anxiety, he left the firm for another company.

The Truth Is . . .

The only thing we have to fear is fear itself.
— Franklin D. Roosevelt

- You can't escape from yourself.

- Your fears are among your greatest teachers.

- When you hear yourself lie, you're speaking out of fear.

- Your lies control your life.

Reflections

When I was younger, I could remember anything,
whether it had happened or not.
— Mark Twain

1. Recall a time in your life when you were trying to run away from a fear, but ran right into it instead.

2. Recall a lie you told recently, and ask yourself what fear motivated you to avoid the truth.

3. Think of an example of a lie you've told that took over your life in some way, for some period of time.

4. Recall a lie about which you feel guilty. Think of at least one thing you learned as a result of that experience.

Realizations

We are so accustomed to wearing a disguise before others
that eventually we are unable to recognize ourselves.
— François, Duc de la Rochefoucauld

1. List three situations, events, or truths that you're trying to run away from.

2. Circle the one that you feel is hurting your life the most.

3. Write ten benefits and ten drawbacks associated with this fear.

4. Open your heart to loving the lessons that the fear offers you, and write a note thanking yourself for seeing in balance the benefits and drawbacks of your fear. Even fear and lies eventually direct you to truth.

Affirmations

- *I am grateful for the opportunities my fears attract because they help me learn unconditional love.*

- *I am grateful equally for my courage and for my fear.*

- *I am facing my fears and loving the lessons of my limitations.*

- *I am listening to the fears of my body and learning to love the wisdom hidden in their messages.*

- *I am opening my heart to the love in the present moment.*

Chapter 21

The Quality of Your Life Depends on the Quality of the Questions You Ask

To find yourself, think for yourself.
— Socrates

Who Are You . . . and Why Are You Here Now?

While many people have discovered who they are and why they're here, most people still look for those answers. Discovering these answers can help your mind and body heal. Since the earliest recorded history, people have been asking four fundamental questions:

- Who am I?
- Why am I here?
- Where did I come from?
- Where am I going?

Our individual beliefs, or our answers to these questions, set the foundation for the other questions we ask, and it appears that the quality of our questions determines that of our lives.

If you believe that you're a mere mortal, then your questions and vision for life will be limited by mortality. If you believe your true essence is an immortal soul, then your questions and vision for life are expansive and immortal. People with immortal vision see beyond the boundaries that many other humans construct. They're often the ones responsible for great discoveries and innovations and making lasting differences in the world. They ask themselves wise and stimulating questions—and they believe that they can find the answers.

When Albert Einstein was only 16 years old, he asked himself the question, *What would the universe look like riding on a beam of light?* That question eventually led to his theory of relativity, which changed the way we think of energy, time, and space. When Elizabeth Blackwell questioned why all physicians were men and decided there was no real reason for it, she enrolled in medical college and, in 1849, became the first woman in the United States to be granted a medical degree. Orville and Wilbur Wright pondered the idea of making a machine that could take people into the air; they went on to invent the first American airplane. These are just three of the myriad examples of people who asked questions that probed deeper and further than others had before.

Many of today's most brilliant minds have been posing intriguing questions and finding profound answers that affect our world and how we see ourselves. Deep questioning led to the theory that consciousness is a cloud of charged particles of light. A number of physicists consider their studies in some ways to be akin to certain areas of theology, and that immortality can be proven scientifically. Years ago, many might have scoffed at these conclusions, and some certainly still do today. But those who listen to their inner voice and follow the quest initiated by their questions are finding inspiring answers that lead to even more inspiring and stimulating questions.

Your Questions Direct Your Learning

It's important that students bring a certain ragamuffin, barefoot irreverence to their studies; they are not here to worship what is known, but to question it.
— Jacob Bronowski

- You learn about the people, places, things, events, beliefs, and ideas that you question.

- Your questions are sparked by your purpose.

- Your soul encourages you to learn about whatever you find most inspiring.

- To stretch your mind, ponder the imponderable.

The questions you ask indicate what you want to learn, and the questions that inspire you stem from your heart and soul. That's why discovering what you love to learn can help you unveil your life's purpose, and finding your purpose will help you understand who you are, where you're going, and why you're here.

The more you stretch your mind, the more you develop your ability to imagine, and the more you can ultimately discover. Your mind is stretched by going beyond what appears to be, to examine and appreciate what is. In fact, it's that type of looking and questioning that eventually led me to create The Demartini Method. I was determined to expand beyond the edge of existing theories and develop a reproducible method or science of opening our hearts to the true wisdom of our souls. I envisioned a Method that would enable people to make quantum leaps in their personal growth and transformation. My questions inspired me to delve wholeheartedly into my research and reading in a variety of disciplines, including biology, biophysics, mathematics, and chemistry. I was also fascinated by genetics, psychology, theology, and astronomy; and my inner voice insisted that all true sciences and religions are linked by some common thread. I studied and linked information from the various sciences day and night, literally reading everything I could get my hands on.

During those intense hours of study, I came across quantities of wonderful research on the topics of gravity, electromagnetism, and nuclear forces, all under the grand topic of quantum physics. Much of what I read referred to the "collapsing" of wave or particle functions. For some reason, the term *collapse* had a special meaning for me. When I looked at this further, I finally understood and truly appreciated the advanced wisdom of the ancient hermetics, who understood the universal laws of complementary order and harmony. These same laws formed the basis for The Demartini Method—formerly The Quantum Collapse Process.

When I discovered that The Demartini Method could bring what appears to be disharmony and chaos into perfect harmony and order, and give birth to the lightness of unconditional love, I literally experienced tears of gratitude. Today I'm grateful to have the opportunity to share The Demartini Method with others. Each time someone's heart opens to the wisdom and lightness of their soul, and they experience the harmony of unconditional love, I'm thankful.

Examine Your Beliefs

If you'd be a real seeker after truth, it's necessary that at least once in your life, you doubt, as far as possible, all things.
— René Descartes

- Many of your beliefs were formed before you were old enough to know that you were learning a mixture of theory and truth.

- When you follow your beliefs back to their roots, you gain a clearer perspective of your foundation.

- Question the statements that you automatically accept as true.

- Pursue the inspired questions of your heart and soul.

Many of the beliefs that have the greatest impact on our lives have been passed down from generation to generation. In fact, if you examine your beliefs, chances are you'll realize that you don't know why you believe some of them. You probably don't remember how or when you began believing some of the others. When you question your beliefs, you educate yourself and gain clarity and certainty. You also give yourself the opportunity to see and step beyond the beliefs, situations, and relationships that aren't based on truth.

Many years ago, at the entrance to the library at Wharton College, I met a man passing out religious pamphlets to teach people about his beliefs and try to convert them to his religion. As I was about to enter the library to study copies of the original writings of Gandhi, this man approached me and asked me not to go inside.

When I asked him why not, he said, "A library is an evil place. To go into this building is to enter the devil's chamber. The only book you ever need to read is the Bible. I've read all those other books, and they were of no use."

I asked this man, who couldn't have been more than 20 years old, how he was able to read all the books in the library so quickly and come to his conclusion. "That's not important," he replied. Something about the way he responded made me question if he had even read the entire Bible—a significant question, since it revealed to me the value of not limiting myself in my investigations. It also inspired me to question and research deeply many sciences, philosophies, and theologies; and it stimulated my interest to reread the Bible. I learned, with certainty, that one inspired question leads to another, and these questions continue to direct my most profound learning.

The Truth Is . . .

A man should look for what is,
and not for what he thinks should be.
— Albert Einstein

- Your questions forge the direction of your quest.

- When you examine your beliefs, you gain clarity and certainty.

- One inspired question leads to another.

- Great truths are ridiculed and opposed before they eventually come to be accepted as obvious.

Reflections

Your questions indicate the depth of your belief.
Look at the depth of your questions.
— John and Lyn St. Clair Thomas

1. Recall a belief you once professed but no longer hold to be true.

2. Think of a statement that you believe to be "obviously true" and ask yourself why you believe it.

3. Think of something you considered to be a fact and passed along to others, only to find out later that it was false.

4. Recall a question about which you have often wondered, and commit at least one hour of reading or research to an investigation of the answer.

Realizations

*Seek always for the answer within. Be not influenced
by those around you, by their thoughts or their words.*
— Eileen Caddy

Write out your three strongest beliefs. Below each,
explain why you believe it and note when you began
believing it.

Affirmations

- *I learn about my inspired questions.*

- *I ponder the imponderable to stretch my mind.*

- *I examine my beliefs and open my heart to the
  wisdom of my soul.*

- *I am grateful for the questions that result from
  physical illness and mental stress because I know
  that they are messages from my heart and soul.*

- *I know that the answer to all great questions is
  unconditional love.*

Chapter 22

Nothing in Life Has Any Meaning, Except the Meaning You Give it

There is no meaning to life except the meaning man gives his life
by the unfolding of his powers, by living productively.
— Erich Fromm

What's the Meaning of This?

From the moment we're born, we observe and analyze our surroundings. We begin making decisions based on those observations and whatever else we perceive with our senses. That's why people's perspectives are so different. Even when several people experience the exact same event, each one will perceive, interpret, and explain it differently. Thus, the same situation can bring about healing for one person but sickness for another. How could it be any other way?

Your assessment of any specific event in your life will be based on your previous experiences and learning. According to that information, you decide what the event means and often judge it to be good or bad. But if that same event occurs in the life of someone with a different history and perspective, he or she will invest it with an entirely different meaning and judge it in a totally different way.

For example, if you grew up in a family or culture that celebrated and rewarded hunting skills, you might associate good feelings with hunting; if you shoot a deer, you'll probably think of it as a good thing—something to celebrate and feel proud about. But if the family or culture in which you grew up condemned hunting, the thought of shooting a deer might distress you greatly, and even make you feel sick.

I've always enjoyed a story I heard as a boy about a wise Native American medicine man who possessed the ability to balance a situation and see both sides quickly. One day, his village was attacked by another tribe and the medicine man's son broke his leg. The people in the village said this was bad, but the medicine man said, "We'll see."

A few months later, several of his son's friends set out on an excursion to hunt game. They said, "It's too bad his leg is still healing, and he can't go with us on our hunt."

The son agreed, but the wise medicine man said, "We'll see."

Months passed, but the three young braves never returned. The people in the village said, "It's good your son did not go on that hunt." But the medicine man said, "We'll see."

The story continues, but the message remains the same. To reserve judgment and see both sides of a situation in balance is a true sign of wisdom. Since an event seen or experienced by many different people doesn't always mean the same thing to everyone—and can actually mean many different things—we eventually realize that events themselves are neutral. We give them a meaning, or "color," based on what we believe or know. The more we understand, the more we can love.

Your Perceptions Color the Truth

If the doors of perception were cleansed every thing
would appear to man as it is, infinite.
— William Blake

- Perceptions generally are based on a very limited amount of information, especially when compared with the vastness of the universe.

- Your perceptions often exaggerate or minimize the truth.

- A wide variety of perceptions sometimes makes the truth appear relative.

- Your reality is based on your perception of the truth

The truth is not always obvious, especially since we generally see it through the filters of our own perceptions. But the more we learn about different beliefs within our culture, and in other times and cultures, the more we understand and are humbled by the knowledge that our perceptions are based on very narrow, limited views of the universe. The more we see and experience, the more we comprehend that our reality and the meanings we assign to events are individualized according to the time and space in which we live.

If you were a farmer experiencing a drought, you'd welcome rain and see its coming as a good event. But if you were on the roof of a low building as flood waters rose around you, you'd probably dread the rain and see it as bad. The truth is that rain is rain—neither good nor bad. It just is.

I still remember a discussion I had with three other students in one of my literature classes in high school. We were talking about the legend of Robin Hood, and each of us had a different opinion about his actions. What one of us thought was good, someone else thought was bad, and vice versa. Clearly we each had our own perception of the legend and what it meant.

Our teacher overheard our discussion and decided to involve the entire class. He asked us all to write down what we believed to be Robin Hood's best and worst qualities. Out of 20 students, 13 different qualities were listed as his best and 15 different character traits listed as his worst. It was a wonderful lesson in differences in perspective—one that has stayed with me through the years.

Emotions Are Based on Perceptions

Men are disturbed not by things,
but by the views they take of them.
— Epictetus

- How you feel about something or someone is based on your perceptions.

- People often fear and condemn what they don't understand.

- When you feel elated or depressed, you're viewing the situation with lopsided perception.

- Your perceptions of the people and events around you determine your reactions.

Our emotions are important to us. They feel real, and we often attempt to find validation for them. But our emotions are based on our perceptions, which often are lopsided. So we may truly feel a certain way about an event or a person, but that doesn't mean what we feel is the truth!

For example, when you're feeling elated or depressed, you might believe that something or someone is more good than bad, or conversely, more bad than good. But that doesn't mean that it's true.

I recently met George, a middle-aged man who looked old and tired and said he was depressed because his 24-year-old daughter, Kate, "was killing him." When I asked him to tell me about it, he said, "She ran off with some jerk and married him, after I told her that I'd disown her if she kept dating him! I can't believe she did this to me. She's my only daughter, and now I've lost her to that scumbag."

George didn't see that he had a choice in how he was feeling and reacting. He was caught in the illusion that his emotions were the truth. I explained that emotions are based on our perceptions, and that if George were to broaden his perspective, he would probably feel differently.

For the next several hours, I helped George balance his perceptions of his daughter Kate and of Don, his new son-in-law. As we probed deeper and deeper into George's perceptions, he began to realize that one of the reasons he disliked Don so much was because the young man reminded him of Frankie, who had dated Kate's mother before George dated and married her.

"I know what that kind of guy is after," said George. "He wants someone to wait on him hand and foot and look like a trophy all the time so he can brag to his friends. It makes me sick to think he's getting that from my daughter!"

It took some time, but eventually George was able to understand that his opinions and perceptions of Frankie, and the similarities he appeared to have with Don, were coloring his perception. Rather than open his mind and heart to the truth, George believed his emotions. When he truly began to comprehend that he was letting his emotions dictate his reactions, and thereby creating his own heartache, he began to cry, and he humbled himself to the truth. George finally opened his heart and his face began to shine with the lightness of unconditional love. He was speechless for several minutes before he whispered, "Thank you."

The Truth Is . . .

Tragedy and comedy are but two aspects
of what is real, and whether we see the tragic or the
humorous is a matter of perspective.
— Arnold Beisser

- Events are neutral.

- Your perspective determines your perception of reality.

- You assign to people and events meanings based on your previous experiences and knowledge.

- Emotions may feel real, but often they're far from the truth.

Reflections

Things don't change.
You change your way of looking, that's all.
— Carlos Castaneda

1. Recall meeting someone about whom you initially had a bad feeling but later felt good about.

2. Recall an event in your life that appeared to be bad, or to have a bad meaning, which later turned out to seem good or have a good meaning.

3. Think of a principle or practice you condemned when you first heard about it, but later accepted when you acknowledged a bigger picture.

4. Think of a miscommunication that occurred in your life because you believed a certain word or action meant one thing, and the person with whom you were talking believed it meant something else.

Realizations

Look at all the sentences which seem true, and question them.
— David Riesman

1. Imagine that you're about to land on planet Earth and take complete control. Your responsibility is to tell everyone what's good and will be rewarded and what's bad and will be punished. No exceptions will be permitted to the rules you dictate. Write about one event or behavior that will be considered good under all circumstances and one event or behavior that will be considered bad under all circumstances.

2. List three drawbacks to what you just described as all good.

3. List three benefits of whatever you described as all bad.

4. Write about a time when you did or were whatever you deemed to be good—and about a time when you did or were whatever you deemed bad. Focus on one of the seven areas of your life: mental, physical, spiritual, familial, social, vocational, or financial.

There is a balance in each of us, but it takes a true and humbling inspection to discover it.

Affirmations

*   *I keep my heart open to the truth in order to balance my perceptions.*

- *I choose my point of view, my emotions, and my reactions. I am the creator of my reality.*

- *I acknowledge the balance in all people, things, and events, and I know the true meaning of all that exists is love.*

- *My balanced perspective and new meaning for life now heals my mind and body.*

Chapter 23

There Is Nothing to Forgive

*The whole of what we know is a system of
compensations. Each suffering is rewarded; each
sacrifice is made up, every debt is paid.*
— Ralph Waldo Emerson

Do You Know What Truly Is?

In order to forgive someone, you must first judge
something they did as bad or wrong. But to sit in
judgment is to behave as if we know everything there is
to know about a person or a situation. The truth is, we
generally know very little about the big picture or the
grand design. Since all of existence is part of this master
plan, then everything and everyone who exists is a part of
the perfection—even our sickness and disease. In the long
run, there are no actual mistakes.

Our limited vision and self-centered perspectives
may sway us to believe that what we see and experience
is all bad or wrong, but the universe maintains a perfect
balance. Everyone who exists, and everything that occurs,

is an integral part of the master plan to help us learn lessons of unconditional love and realize our own true potential.

When you think about it, who are we to judge the workings of the universe? When we humble ourselves, we clearly comprehend that all of our perceptions, beliefs, knowledge, and wisdom only amount to a grain of sand in the vast ocean of conscious possibilities. That's why it's much wiser to reserve judgment and look for the balance of benefits in every so-called negative person and event that we encounter.

Even the events that seem the most terrible, violent, and senseless are filled with opportunities for us to find the benefits and experience the serenity of unconditional love. The universe is governed by the laws of cause and effect. But life doesn't punish or reward us, and it doesn't condemn or forgive us. We attract the lessons we need to learn and we sow what we reap. We're all on a healing journey of love, and the more we're grateful for the balance of the universe, the more unconditional love we experience, and the sooner we're able to experience the fulfillment of love.

I recently had the opportunity to talk with Hank, whose three-year-old son, Tommy, had been abducted and killed 15 years earlier. Still filled with rage, Hank blamed the man who killed his son, he blamed himself for not being there to protect his son, and he blamed God for letting the whole thing happen. He felt that God had turned His back on him.

I explained to Hank that as long as his heart was filled with anger and blame, he was blocking the love and inner poise that his heart and soul were sending him. I asked if he would like to let go of his anger so that he could experience a more fulfilling state of unconditional love. He said yes.

Hank's first step was to write down all the drawbacks surrounding Tommy's death. He had focused on what he perceived to be bad for many years, so he quickly listed more than 70 such drawbacks. I then asked him to write down an equal number of benefits that resulted from Tommy's death. At first he thought I was kidding, then he became defensive, but as we continued to talk, he saw the value in what I was asking him to do. After about two hours, he had written as many benefits as drawbacks.

I asked if he wanted to share some of the benefits he discovered, and he said, "I was having such a hard time writing down even one benefit that I realized I wasn't letting myself see anything but what I thought was bad. But when I finally pushed myself to write down a benefit, I started to see that there really have been a lot of blessings. Tommy's case got a lot of attention, and people who never even thought about missing children learned how many there are, and how fast it can happen."

He said another benefit was learning that even people who didn't know him cared about him and his family. He received hundreds of cards and letters, and many people sent prayers and messages of love and support. "I've learned to appreciate life and the people I love," he said. "I sure don't take anything for granted anymore. And I guess that's the biggest blessing of all."

Next I asked Hank to look at the 73 items he said were drawbacks, and for each one find an example where he had, in some way, in one of the areas of his life, done the same thing to someone else or to himself. This part of the process took a few hours as Hank looked diligently into his own life and memories. He swore that he had never done a few items, but when we looked more closely, he found matching actions or inactions somewhere in his life, in some form.

The final step was for Hank to look at all the drawbacks he'd listed, and this time find a way that each one of them actually had served him or someone else. Near the end of this process, Hank looked up and said, "You know, I'm finally starting to see some meaning in Tommy's death."

When Hank put down his pen, he didn't need to tell me that he had completed the process. I could see the transition he had experienced. His eyes were brighter, he held his head higher, and his entire physical being appeared to be more relaxed. Hank realized that Tommy's death had just as many hidden benefits as it had drawbacks, and he understood that blame and forgiveness were illusions; the only way to free himself from both was to be grateful and open his heart to the truth of unconditional love.

I asked Hank if there was anything he'd like to say to Tommy in his mind. He closed his eyes for a moment, and then with tears rolling down his face he said, "Tommy, you know I love you, son."

Forgiveness Is a Self-Righteous Illusion

We are members of a vast cosmic orchestra in which each living instrument is essential to the complementary and harmonious playing of the whole.
— J. Allen Boone

- Forgiveness demands a prior judgment of some unethical or immoral action or inaction.

- It's an action of pride and self-righteous ego to think that you have the right to judge or to forgive.

- Forgiving someone won't set them free; it will perpetuate further cycles of judgment and illusions. Only unconditional love can set people free.

- The actual truth requires no forgiveness.

Once we open our heart to the wisdom of our souls, we step into the present moment, experience unconditional love, and understand that all that has occurred is perfection. There's nothing to forgive. The illusion of forgiveness is sometimes a step on the path to unconditional love, but if we stop at forgiveness, we remain in a human state of judgment. We must give up our self-righteous egos and go beyond blame and forgiveness to step into the lightness of unconditional love.

A few years ago, as I was about to discuss the illusion of forgiveness in one of my personal success programs, a participant named David told me that he'd already forgiven his father for all the things he'd "done to him." He said, "I finished forgiving him over a year ago." David explained that he'd been through years of therapy and numerous workshops that helped him accept what his father had done to him and to learn to live with it. "I've already told my dad that even though he was very wrong for abusing me, I've forgiven him," he explained.

I asked David if he'd want to share a hug with his father if he were in the room right now, and he laughed and said,

"I wouldn't go that far! I've forgiven the guy, but after all I've been through, I sure don't feel like hugging him!" I explained to David that if he still misperceived that his dad had done something that needed forgiveness, he was not truly free from himself or his dad. I asked him if he'd like to be truly free, not just in his head, but in his heart. He said that he thought he already was, but would be willing to see if there could be more.

I then explained The Demartini Method to David and he began working on it. About halfway through, I asked if David was beginning to recognize the difference between forgiveness and the true state of unconditional love. He said that he was, and he was very surprised to discover that many of the things for which he was angry at his father, he had done to someone else. He was also surprised to discover some of the very valuable "goods" that arose from what looked like bad actions.

Continuing on The Demartini Method, he finally balanced the goods and bads of his experiences. His heart was filled with love and he began to cry tears of gratitude and inspiration. I asked David if there was someone in the room that reminded him of his father, and he turned to an older man on his right and said that he did. I then asked David if he'd like to share with this man what he'd do and say to his father if he were present. David nodded, and as the other participant turned to face him, David reached out to hug his "dad." With tears streaming down his face, he managed to say "thank you." He thanked him for all the things he learned growing up, for all the strengths he had given him, and just for being his dad.

I asked David if he still felt there was any "wrongdoing" or mistake in the way things had happened. He smiled and said, "For the first time in my life, I know that everything that happened was perfect. Thank you!"

There is a world of difference between so-called forgiveness, with the judgments that accompany it, and the openhearted gratitude that releases unconditional love.

Nothing Can Be Created or Destroyed

> *If you wish to make an apple pie from scratch,*
> *you must first invent the universe.*
> — Carl Sagan

- Every bit of matter that has existed, still exists today.

- Matter can't be created or destroyed; it can only change forms.

- You can't build something up without tearing something down; you can't tear something down without building something up.

We think of ourselves as creating and destroying things, but actually, we can only manipulate or change the form of the matter that already exists. When we manipulate matter, it's impossible to build without tearing down, or tear down without building. When we plant a garden, we "build" a crop. This crop can intentionally be plowed under, but the field itself becomes equally fertile simultaneously. We've neither created nor destroyed anything. We've merely transformed one form of energy and matter into another.

I once had a talk with a little girl named Marsha after

her father buried her dog, Rusty, who had been hit by a car. She was holding Rusty's collar in her hands and crying, but she said, "I'm not crying because Rusty's dead. I know that's just Rusty's body in the ground. The real Rusty can never be dead."

I gave her a big hug and said, "You're very wise, Marsha."

She smiled at me, still crying, and said, "But why do I feel so bad, Dr. Demartini?"

As Marsha and I walked through the garden, we talked about how the flowers and the bees and the butterflies and birds all helped each other out. They were in harmony with each other. I asked Marsha what the garden looked like in the cold winter months, and she frowned and said, "It's ugly. It's just all dirt, with some weeds poking out."

I explained to her that what looked like "just all dirt" was what made flowers grow again in spring. "The flowers drop their seeds in the fall, and their leaves and stems and petals make nutritious fertilizer for the seeds," I said. "The seeds wait patiently in the ground, and then in the spring, they germinate and turn into beautiful flowers again."

"Yeah, I get it." she said, "You mean like the circle of life in *The Lion King*." But she frowned and said, "But Rusty's bones aren't going to turn into another Rusty."

We sat down on a bench and I explained that the physical parts of Rusty's body would nourish new life in other forms, but they couldn't turn into another dog because "the real part of Rusty that you know isn't dead. He'll be alive in your heart as long as you love him."

She nodded her head and said, "Then he'll always be alive. Because I'll always love him."

The Truth Is . . .

The simple-minded use of the notions "right" or "wrong" is one of the chief obstacles to the progress of understanding.
— Alfred North Whitehead

- The universe is governed by the laws of perfect balance.

- The state of unconditional love is beyond blame, and beyond forgiveness.

- To love others with all your mind, heart, and soul is to love for the sake of love.

- The universe doesn't make mistakes.

Reflections

Life and death are one, even as the river and sea are one.
— Kahlil Gibran

1. Recall the person, event, or thing that you most recently judged as all negative and take a moment to see the other side of the illusion.

2. Recall someone whom you vowed you'd never forgive, and consider loving them instead.

3. Think of something or someone you imagined was no longer in existence, and look for where or how they now exist in a new form.

4. Close your eyes and allow yourself to remember that you're one with all that exists.

Realizations

If God be for us, who can be against us?
— Romans 8:31

1. On a sheet of paper, write the initials of someone toward whom you feel anger or other negative emotions.

2. Next, write 15 things you perceive as bad or wrong about that person. Then write down one way in which you have done the equivalent of each of those things to someone else. Finally, write one way that each of your perceived negatives has been a blessing.

3. Write a letter to this person, expressing heartfelt gratitude for their perfection in the universe.

4. Ask your heart for any message of love.

Affirmations

- *I am grateful for the grand and masterful design.*

- *I know there is a perfect balance, even when I don't see it.*

- *Every person and every event provides an opportunity for me to learn another lesson in unconditional love.*

- *When I miss someone, I open my heart and remember that they are still here—and simply have changed form.*

- *I am healed and my heart is open.*

Chapter 24

Your Heart
and Soul Have the
Wisdom of the Ages

All learning is recollection.
— Plato

Are You Online with the Universal Design?

Global communications systems and technological advances now give people state-of-the-art access to a previously undreamed of world of information. Everyone talks about the Web, the Internet, and e-mail. While these systems are marvelous inventions and innovations, they can't match your heart and soul's abilities to tune in to universal knowledge and the wisdom of the ages.

Your heart and soul are your true, inner essence. They're your connection to the source of who you really are. Your open heart doesn't recognize the illusions of boundaries that your human eyes see between people and other things. Your soul is one with all that has evolved—one with all creation. Your soul knows what was, what is, and what will be in the course of your journey.

When you're truly grateful, your mind is still and your heart is open. You can hear the messages of love and guidance that your soul is sending to you. This inner voice, especially the voice that speaks when you're in a state of deep inspiration, is worthy of your attention. Part of wisdom is listening to the voice of your soul and obeying what it's telling you. The more effectively you quiet the chattering voices of your mental fragments, the more clearly you'll be able to hear the one true voice of your soul.

Everyone has the innate ability to listen to their soul and follow its inspiration, but few actually choose to follow this enlightened path earnestly. That's why the highest truths are generally comprehended by the few—not the many.

I clearly remember the day about 12 years ago when, during a meditation, my inner voice revealed to me a message that instantly brought tears of inspiration. My inner voice said that I was to build a school. In fact, this voice provided me with the name for the school—the Concourse of Wisdom.

At that time, The Demartini Method had yet to be formalized, and my teaching skills were in their infancy. But the inspiration and voice were so strong that I followed them and began teaching courses on the two topics I knew the most about—unconditional love and healing.

A few years after I built the philosophical foundation for the Concourse of Wisdom, I refined The Demartini Method and determined that I was ready to begin teaching it as part of The Breakthrough Experience. Today, the Concourse of Wisdom supports an international body of students, and it offers numerous courses that merge together the sciences and philosophies of health. When you follow the inspirations of your heart and soul, you fulfill your life's true mission.

Your Soul Speaks When You're Grateful for What Is, as It Is

> *Depend more upon the intuitive forces from within, and not harken so much to outside influences, but learn to listen to the still, small voice within.*
> — Edgar Cayce

- True, heartfelt gratitude opens the lines of communication with your soul.

- Emotional charges create static interference in the connection with your soul.

- When your heart is open and you're thankful for the perfection of the universe, your soul often responds with a message of unconditional love.

- Gratefulness releases your soul's guidance and its true power of healing—unconditional love.

When you're truly grateful for what is, as it is, your heart and soul speak to you and guide you with inspired questions, ideas, and visions for the future. Even when you're not grateful, your heart and soul speak to you, but you can't always hear them when you're caught up with the many voices and directions of your various interests and responsibilities. That's why it's important to set aside time to be grateful. Taking just five minutes in the morning and five minutes in the evening to be deeply thankful for all the blessings in your life can keep the lines of communication with your heart and soul clear.

I've been gifted with the opportunity to hear many of the inspirations people have had during and after these moments of true gratitude. I'm certain that we can learn our soul's ultimate mission and purpose simply by being grateful for what is, as it is. I'm also certain that our hearts and souls can give us the information and guidance needed to improve our lives and to heal our minds and bodies.

When I think about the major impact that gratitude has on people's lives, I often think of a chiropractic patient of mine many years ago. Janice came to my office because she had been injured in an automobile accident. The first four or five times she came in for an adjustment, she complained during most of her appointment. I knew that her ingratitude was blocking the healing process, and I knew I'd truly love to help her.

The next time she came in, before she had an opportunity to begin focusing on her perceived negatives, I told her that I was doing an experiment and asked if she would mind listing 20 things for which she was grateful before I performed her adjustment.

About ten minutes later, when she'd finished her list, she came into the treatment room and handed it to me with a smile. I then explained to her that her adjustment could be more helpful if we remained silent and focused on the effects we desired from the healing.

We continued this procedure for several weeks, and Janice noticed a remarkable improvement in her back's flexibility and level of comfort. She also mentioned that she was beginning to have more energy, which she believed resulted from her adjustments. I acknowledged that the adjustments were making a difference, but I also explained that I believed her gratitude was speeding her recovery.

Janice was intrigued by this and wondered what might happen if she made a list of 20 things she was grateful for every day, instead of just once a week when she came for her appointment. She committed to focusing on the blessings in her life and on her vision of a healthy, strong back every day. Within five weeks, Janice's back no longer had any swelling, and her flexibility was completely restored.

When You Obey Your Heart and Soul's Guidance, Your Life Becomes Fulfilled

Conscience: that little spark of celestial fire.
— George Washington

- A master of complete health has the discipline to listen to his or her heart and soul.

- A genius is one who listens to and obeys the wisdom of his or her soul.

- Your heart and soul most desire to fulfill their healing mission of love.

- The heart and soul express only unconditional love.

Your heart and soul form your internal guiding system. When you humble yourself with gratitude, you tap in to their guidance and begin to fulfill your life's mission. While this might sound mysterious, it's actually very simple. It's just a matter of allowing the energy and lightness of unconditional love to flow through you, instead of blocking it with unbalanced emotions and brain noise.

Several years ago, I met an inspired sculptor. Jason had felt that he'd been called to create masterpieces of art. Then 27 years old, from the time Jason had graduated from high school until he was 22, he'd worked in a Manhattan garage parking cars. On his days off, however, he'd visit as many museums, art galleries, and exhibits as he had time for and could afford.

"One day, as I was admiring an exquisite sculpture of a dolphin," he said, "I began to imagine that my hands had created it. I could dearly see the vision of my talent, and I felt called to pursue this art." After that day, he knew that he could create sculpture that people would admire and appreciate as much as he appreciated the dolphin.

Jason began taking classes at a nearby art school. He loved the texture of the sculpting clay, and he loved being able to create whatever he could imagine. The more he practiced, the more his talent unfolded, and within three years of the day he had his vision of sculpting, his work was displayed in a local gallery for the first time.

"I'm so grateful for following that vision I had at the museum of art," he said. "After that, I knew what I loved to do, and I knew that I could somehow do it. I believed it, I saw it, and it happened."

The Truth Is . . .

Until you know that life is inspiring, and find it so,
you haven't found the message of your soul.
— Anonymous

- When you're grateful for what is, as it is, you open your heart to the wisdom of your soul.

- Your soul is one with all that exists.

- Your soul is your true and lasting essence.

- When you obey the wisdom of your heart and soul, you fulfill your life's mission.

Reflections

Dust thou art, to dust returnest,
Was not spoken of the soul.
— Henry Wadsworth Longfellow

1. Close your eyes and think of all the things in your life for which you feel truly grateful.

2. Thank yourself for acknowledging these great blessings.

3. Thank your heart and soul for their love, and listen for an inspired message.

4. Write a thank-you note to someone you love.

Realizations

For what is a man profited, if he shall
gain the whole world and lose his own soul?
— Matthew 16:26

1. Think of a situation or health condition about which you'd love to have your heart and soul's guidance. Write it on a sheet of paper.

2. Next, write ten advantages of the situation or condition—ten ways it has served or benefited you.

3. Thank your heart and soul for the benefits of your situation or condition. Keep thanking until tears of gratitude come to your eyes.

4. Ask your heart and soul for guidance, and write down your inspired message.

Affirmations

- *I am disciplined to follow my healing heart and soul.*

- *I obey my heart and soul's loving guidance gratefully.*

- *I open my heart to the wisdom of the ages.*

- *I am a cup filled with love and gratitude.*

- *I am grateful for the healing guidance of my heart and soul, and I apply it in my daily life.*

Chapter 25

Unconditional Love Is the Key to Your Heart and Soul

*Love gives naught but itself, and takes naught
but from itself. Love possesses not, nor would it be
possessed. For love is sufficient unto love.*
— Kahlil Gibran

Would You Love to Hear Your Heart?

Most people want to experience the openhearted
state of unconditional love—not only for others,
but for themselves—more than anything else in the world.
But there's a vast difference between the passionate
emotion called infatuation that many people call love and
commonly experience, and true, unconditional love.

Unconditional love isn't just a passion or positive
emotion at all. It's a complete merging of all emotions,
positive and negative. It takes you to a state of inspiration.
It occurs when you step into the present moment and
become awakened by the visions and messages of your

heart and soul. It's your link to that feeling of eternal life and your guide to acknowledging the magnificent universe.

Unconditional love is the greatest force in existence. It has no boundaries, limitations, or opposition. It's the alpha and the omega—the beginning and the end. It embraces everyone and everything equally. Neither positive nor negative, it's the energy and light that's born when positive and negative emotional charges are perfectly balanced.

It was due to the realization of the profundity of this force that I was inspired to create The Demartini Method, the science that balances the positives and negatives step-by-step and leads people into a state of gratitude, where their hearts open, and they experience the intensity and power of unconditional love. The exercises throughout this book have been designed to help you balance your perceptions and emotional charges so that you can experience the wisdom and sacred healing that unconditional love offers at every moment.

Because of The Demartini Method, I've been blessed to experience the awe of unconditional love many times in my life. My greatest fulfillment is derived from passing this torch to others, and in return, being blessed with the opportunity to experience more unconditional love in my own life. We all possess the ability to reach this state of openheartedness, and we all have an inner urge that propels us to seek this truth.

I remember one of the first times I offered The Demartini Method, during The Breakthrough Experience. Twelve participants were seated around a conference table, each of whom introduced him- or herself and gave a little bit of personal background. When we reached the last person, Mark, who was seated to my left, he said,

"I'm here because I hate my mother, I hate myself, and my whole life has been about hate . . . and all I want is to be loved." Then he began to cry; not just a few tears, but a sobbing outpouring of emotion.

I asked Mark if he'd like to share his story, and in a very detached manner, he began to tell us the details of his life:

> Well, let's see. When I was born, my mother threw me away in a hospital trash can. But I cried loudly enough that the nurses found me. After a few weeks in the hospital, someone decided that my mother had to keep me, so they gave me back to her, even though she said that she didn't want me.

He explained that over the next ten years, he experienced what he considered repeated abuse from his mother and was bounced back and forth between her, foster homes, hospitals, and eventually the juvenile detention center. His mother tried to suffocate him, burned him with cigarettes, locked him in his bedroom closet, and never hugged him or told him that she loved him. In fact, she told him that she hated him and that he'd ruined her life.

When Mark finished his story, a heavy silence hung in the room. I thanked Mark for being willing to share his story and told him with certainty that before the end of the program, he'd experience the unconditional love for which he yearned, and he'd thank his mother for her contribution to his life.

I know that he didn't believe me at that time, but he hung in there, and when we began The Demartini Method later that day, he was the most anxious to get started. In less than two hours, Mark wrote more than five pages of perceived negatives about his mother. When I explained that the next step was to find a positive for each of the negatives, he accused me of being a wishful thinker and threatened to walk out of the program, but he decided to stay and follow through on the process.

When I looked at Mark's Demartini Method forms a few hours later, I saw that he'd written almost as many perceived positives as negatives, with only about 20 to go to balance his columns. I asked him what he was finding out about himself.

"I gotta tell you," he said, "this is harder than anything I've ever done. I didn't think there was one single good thing about my mother, and in the last few hours, I've actually recalled some great memories, and even laughed out loud a few times about some of the funny things she used to say."

I knew that Mark was beginning to gain some balance in his perceptions, but I also knew that he held a great deal of anger toward his mother, and anger blocks unconditional love.

When Mark had balanced his columns of perceived negatives and positives, I asked him to go back to the negative column and find three examples in his own life when he'd done to someone else the same thing that his mother had done to him. I explained that he would be wise to look into all seven areas of his life—physical, mental, financial, spiritual, familial, social, and vocational—to find these examples.

About an hour into this part of the process, Mark said that he had a few things on his list that his mother had done that he was sure he never did. When I asked him to give me an example, he said, "I never threw away my own baby!" I asked Mark how he felt when he thought about his mother putting him in the trash can. He said that he felt anger and rejection. So I asked him when he had made someone else feel angry and rejected. Though he claimed he never had, as we looked for this example in the other areas of his life, Mark mentioned a woman named Mariel to whom he had been engaged to be married a few a years before. It didn't work out.

I sensed this was the example we were looking for, and asked Mark why it didn't work out. "I don't know," he said. "She was great, and I blew it." I asked him to explain how he "blew it," and he said, "I got scared and broke off our engagement just a few weeks before the wedding. She accused me of dumping her at the altar, and I haven't seen her or talked to her since." When I asked Mark if he had loved Mariel, he said that he still did.

"So you loved her, and you dumped her because you were scared," I observed. He nodded. I asked softly; "Did she feel angry and rejected the way you did when you discovered that your mother dumped you?"

Mark's eyes opened wide, and all he could say was, "Oh my God." Throughout the day, several other items came up that Mark didn't believe he had done. But each time, he found a correlation somewhere in his life, and by the end of the day, he was able to see how all of his perceived negatives had in some way served him, and were blessings. Mark acknowledged that he had also done all of the things for which he was angry at his mother, and he was able to see that his mother actually had as many positive traits as negative ones.

When he completed his list of all these factors and created a perfect balance in his emotional charges, he broke through more than 15 years of feelings and stepped into the unconditional love of his open heart. He became thankful for his life, and everyone in the room began to cry tears of inspiration and gratitude with him as we all felt the power of the unconditional love that flowed through him. When he said, "Thank God for my mother," whom he'd hated only hours earlier, he actually glowed.

Gratitude Opens Your Heart

To love and be loved is to feel the sun from both sides.
— David Viscott

- Emotional charges and lopsided perceptions create ingratitude.

- The more grateful you are, the wider your heart opens.

- To the degree that you have an open heart, you have no limitations or boundaries.

Many people understand that unconditional love flows through an open heart. But few people are grateful enough to open their hearts instantly whenever they choose. In fact, for most people, the openhearted moments in their lives probably seem to happen magically when they experience a great surge of gratitude. Some of the grateful moments that inspire hearts to open are the birth of a baby, hugging a loved one who has returned home safely, escaping injury or the transition called death in what feels like a near miss, and experiencing new vitality after a successful healing.

But we don't need to wait for those moments to occur. We can create them by focusing on our blessings, the magnificence of this spectacular universe, and the wonder of life itself. Gratitude attracts more gratitude, just like ingratitude attracts more ingratitude. In other words, the more we focus on our blessings, the more blessings we have to focus on, and the more grateful we become.

I received the following letter from a woman who learned how to open her heart with gratitude when she attended The Breakthrough Experience a few years ago. While this is just one of many such letters, it sums up the value of focusing on gratitude and opening your heart.

> *Dear Dr. Demartini,*
>
> *Since learning The Demartini Method, my perceptions of life have gradually changed to a wonderful understanding. When I completed it, I had no idea of the transformation that was to take place. For the first time, I could truly understand and define unconditional love.*
>
> *Now I know that unconditional love is the embracing of each person, persona, and event with acceptance, compassion, and the knowledge that they're here for me, to help me achieve my ultimate purpose. There are no mistakes.*
>
> *To transform your perceptions by doing The Method is to transcend time and space. By working The Method on past and present relationships, I've been able to create the deepest love and understanding I've ever had in my life. My love for these people and events in my life has broadened greatly. However, more astonishing is the reverence, humbleness, and love I've found for God and the universe.*
>
> *Because I began to engulf these transformations and experience my open heart, I began to realize that my life has a grand purpose, and the love I have for myself, others,*

and God will transform my life forever. Thanks to you and the universe for this wonderful vehicle of transformation, for now all of us can truly become responsible for creating unconditional love in our lives.

Love,
Luanne

Unconditional Love Is the Greatest Force in the Universe

Love conquers all.
— Virgil

- Unconditional love brings whomever you love into your presence.

- Unconditional love is the answer to all great questions.

- Unconditional love dissolves the emotional charges that create sickness and disease.

- Unconditional love heals.

Unconditional love takes you beyond the illusions of space and time and helps you bring whomever you love into your presence. That doesn't mean the physical aspect of the person appears; rather, unconditional love flows between you and that person and connects your heart and soul with theirs.

Unconditional love isn't limited by the boundaries of time and space that our physical bodies inhabit. It's a state of awakening and enlightenment that gives rise to the answers to all questions. It's our reason for being here in physical form. We're here to learn unconditional love and can find it in bliss or the long and hard way. Either way, we'll learn it because our evolution back to the very source of life is inevitable.

Unconditional love is the fundamental law and the most powerful force in the universe. It's our link to all true healing and our bond with the infinite. It's our mission, purpose, and stairway to the stars.

When I was young, I spent hours staring at the stars, wondering about why I was here and what it all meant. I was fascinated with the workings of the universe and felt convinced that there was some form of real magic that could conquer all. At that time in my life, I was looking for magical forces in the world around me. Today I know the supreme magical force—that of unconditional love—is within me, you, and everyone and everything that exists.

The Truth Is . . .

We're all in this together—by ourselves.
— Lily Tomlin

- You're one with everything and everyone that exists.

- When you're truly grateful, you transcend the illusions of space and time and soar with your heart and soul.

- Unconditional love is the heart's truth, which runs through all true science and religion.

- Unconditional love is all knowing, all healing, and all powerful.

Reflections

The wise want love; and those who love, want wisdom.
— Percy Bysshe Shelley

1. Recall a moment when your heart was open and you felt the force of unconditional love.

2 Close your eyes and slowly relive that moment in as much detail as you can remember.

3. Review the physical, mental, and spiritual sensations you experienced before, during, and after your heart opened.

4. Stand up and let your arms hang relaxed at your sides. Tip your head back slightly and look toward the sky or ceiling. Gently close your eyes, and silently and inwardly begin being thankful for the openhearted experience you've just recalled.

Thank all the people who have helped you become who you are today. Continue this thankfulness until your heart opens and you feel a state of unconditional love. Then be silent and listen for your heart and soul's inner voices and guidance.

Realizations

Owe no man any thing, but to love one another: for he that loveth another hath fulfilled the law.
— Romans 13:8

1. Write the initials of someone for whom you'd like to have more love.

2. List all the traits about that person you consider to be negative and all the traits you consider positive. Once you've listed the exact same number of positives and negatives, go on to the next step.

3. For every negative and every positive you listed, write at least one example from your own life when you've done the same thing or displayed the same trait.

4. Write a letter of thanks to that person, and continue writing and thanking him or her until your heart opens, you experience tears of inspiration, and you feel the force of unconditional love.

Affirmations

- *I am one with everything and everyone that exists.*

- *I am grateful for what is, as it is.*

- *I am opening my heart to the healing power of unconditional love.*

- *I soar with my heart and soul on the wings of love.*

- *I am now healed.*

Conclusion

*The most beautiful and profound emotion we can experience
is the sensation of the mystical. It is the dower of all true
science. He to whom this emotion is a stranger, who can no
longer wonder and stand rapt in awe, is as good as dead.
To know that what is impenetrable to us really exists,
manifesting itself as the highest wisdom and the most radiant
beauty which our dull faculties can comprehend only in their
most primitive forms—this knowledge, this feeling, is at the
center of true religiousness.*
— Albert Einstein

May you stand rapt in awe at the perfection and magnificence of this universe.

May you listen to the wisdom of your heart and soul and obey.

May you experience the blessings and healing power of the greatest force of all—unconditional love.

May you be thankful and be healed. Thank you.

— Dr. John F. Demartini

Sources

To protect the privacy of Dr. Demartini's clients, some of their names have been changed in the stories that are shared in this book. For kindly granting permission to reprint copyrighted material from the following books, the author thanks their respective publishers:

Brian Adams, *How to Succeed.* North Hollywood, Cal.: Wilshire Book Co., 1985.

Robert Fitzhenry and Anthony Barker, *The Book of Quotations.* New South Wales, Australia: Allen and Unwin, 1994.

Kahlil Gibran, *The Prophet.* Copyright © 1923 by Kahlil Gibran; renewed 1951 by Administrators CTA of Kahlil Gibran Estate and Mary G. Gibran.

Allen Klein, *Quotations to Cheer You up When the World Is Getting You Down.* New York: Sterling, 1991.

Kent Nerburn and Louise Menglekoch, eds. *Native American Wisdom.* San Rafael, Cal.: New World Library, 1991.

William Poole, *The Heart of Healing.* Atlanta: Turner Publishing, 1993.

Every effort has been made to ensure that each author, editor, and publisher has been properly acknowledged, although some sources were not traceable.

AckNowLedgMENts

Thank you to my beautiful late wife, Athena, for her patience, her inspiration, and her love.

Thank you to one of my first mentors, Dr. Paul Bragg, who encouraged me to listen to the inner whisper of my heart and soul, and obey.

Thank you to my publicist, Annie Jennings, for believing in my message of gratitude and love and helping me share it with others.

Thank you to my editor, Toni Robino, for her creative inspirations, her understanding of universal principles, and her love for the philosophy presented in this book.

Thank you to the entire team at Hay House for their commitment to excellence.

About the Author

Dr. John F. Demartini is a professional speaker, author, and business consultant whose clients range from Wall Street financiers, financial planners, and corporate executives to health-care professionals, actors, and sports personalities. The author of *The Breakthrough Experience, How to Make One Hell of a Profit and Still Get to Heaven,* and *You Can Have an Amazing Life . . . in Just 60 Days!,* and founder of the Concourse of Wisdom School of Philosophy and Healing, Dr. Demartini began his career as a doctor of chiropractic and went on to explore more than 200 different disciplines in pursuit of what he calls Universal Principles of Life and Health. As an international speaker, he breathes new life into audiences all over the world with his enlightening perspectives, humorous observations of human nature, and practical action steps.

Website: **www.DrDemartini.com**

Hay House Titles
of Related Interest

Books

Attitude Is Everything for Success, by Keith D. Harrell

Gratitude, by Louise L. Hay and Friends

Inner Peace for Busy People, by Joan Z. Borysenko, Ph.D.

Life Is Short—Wear Your Party Pants, by Lorella LaRoche

Life's a Journey—Not a Sprint, by Jennifer Lewis-Hall

Simple Things, by Jim Brickman, with Cindy Pearlman

10 Secrets for Success and Inner Peace, by Dr. Wayne W. Dyer

All of the above are available at your
local bookstore, or may be ordered by visiting Hay House
(see next page).

We hope you enjoyed this Hay House book.
If you'd like to receive a free catalog featuring additional
Hay House books and products, or if you'd like information about
the Hay Foundation, please contact:

Hay House, Inc.
P.O. Box 5100
Carlsbad, CA 92018-5100

(760) 431-7695 or **(800) 654-5126**
(760) 431-6948 (fax) or **(800) 650-5115 (fax)**
www.hayhouse.com® • **www.hayfoundation.org**

Published and distributed in Australia by: Hay House Australia Pty. Ltd. 18/36
Ralph St. • Alexandria NSW 2015 • *Phone:* 612-9669-4299
Fax: 612-9669-4144 • www.hayhouse.com.au

Published and distributed in the United Kingdom by: Hay House UK, Ltd
292B Kensal Rd., London W10 5BE • *Phone:* 44-20-8962-1230 • *Fax:* 44-20-
8962-1239 • www.hayhouse.co.uk

Published and distributed in the Republic of South Africa by: Hay House SA
(Pty), Ltd., P.O. Box 990, Witkoppen 2068 • *Phone/Fax:* 27-11-706-6612
orders@psdprom.co.za

Published in India by: Hay House Publications (India) Pvt. Ltd., 3 Hampton
Court, A-Wing, 123 Wodehouse Rd., Colaba, Mumbai 400005
Phone: 91 (22) 22150557 or 22180533 • *Fax:* 91 (22) 22839619
www.hayhouseindia.co.in

Distributed in India by: Media Star, 7 Vaswani Mansion, 120 Dinshaw Vachha
Rd., Churchgate, Mumbai 400020 • *Phone:* 91 (22) 22815538-39-40
Fax: 91 (22) 22839619 • booksdivision@mediastar.co.in

Distributed in Canada by: Raincoast • 9050 Shaughnessy St., Vancouver, B.C.
V6P 6E5 • *Phone:* (604) 323-7100 • *Fax:* (604) 323-2600 • www.raincoast.com

Tune in to **HayHouseRadio.com®** for the best
in inspirational talk radio featuring top Hapy House authors!
And, sign up via the Hay House USA Website to receive the Hay
House online newsletter and stay informed about what's going on
with your favorite authors. You'll receive bimonthly announcements
about: Discounts and Offers, Special Events, Product Highlights,
Free Excerpts, Giveaways, and more!
www.hayhouse.com®